LIBERTY IN JESUS!

Evil Spirits and Exorcism
Simply Explained...

'For he has rescued us from the dominion of darkness...' (Col. 1:13)

Liberty in Jesus!

*Evil Spirits and Exorcism
Simply Explained...*

By L. David Mitchell

The Pentland Press Ltd
Edinburgh · Cambridge · Durham · USA

© L. David Mitchell 1999

First published in 1999 by
The Pentland Press Ltd.
1 Hutton Close
South Church
Bishop Auckland
Durham

British Library Cataloguing in Publication Data.
A catalogue record for this book is available
from the British Library.

ISBN 1 85821 611 7

Typeset by George Wishart & Associates, Whitley Bay.
Printed and bound by Antony Rowe Ltd., Chippenham.

To Delphine –
beloved partner all along the Way.

Contents

Foreword

$\mathfrak{J}$ am glad to commend this book by one of God's choice servants, whom I have known for seventeen years. Dr David Mitchell and his godly wife, Delphine, have served with distinction in several churches in the Christian and Missionary Alliance in Canada. During this time he has also been a valued member of our National Board of Directors.

His ministry among us has been marked by the supernatural. Wherever he has served, his ministry has always been in demand beyond his own parish. This quiet, godly man has served his flock and beyond in an unassuming manner, thus allowing Christ to be glorified. In his current status as Minister at Large, his ministry embraces a growing number of other traditions.

I have read this work with interest and with a critical eye, cognizant that this material is not in the regular line of evangelical testimonies. Although David came into our denomination from another tradition, he has modeled for us the signs, wonders and miracles which were commonplace in earlier Alliance history, but are currently more and more infrequent. It was John Wesley who said that some truths have been hidden so long that when they are rediscovered, they sound like heresy.

Liberty in Jesus should be a significant contribution to the renewal of North American Evangelicalism. Without the frequent manifestation of the supernatural in the daily life of our churches, we will fail to pass a vibrant Christian faith on to the next generation.

Arnold L. Cook, President
The Christian and Missionary Alliance in Canada.

Author's Preface

'There's victory in Jesus!' This is the chorus in the old song that Christians often sing with delight, exuberance and gusto! We can fill our lungs and rejoice in all that Christ's triumph means to us, personally.

Whenever I feel the pressure of life getting to me, I make the effort to stand back and get a grip of my feelings long enough to lift up my heart in praise to the Lord. For he is ever present to confirm his victory for me over my circumstances, as well as sin, death and disease. The grace of the Holy Spirit assures me of the truth of the power of his blessed Name and the effectiveness of his precious Blood, and my heavy heart is immediately lightened. I know myself to be a blessed man.

This explains our title, *Liberty in Jesus!* It has the same tune! And it can be sung with the same vim and vigour, by anyone who has ever found that the Holy Name and precious Blood have freed them from spiritual problems which otherwise were beyond solution. This book is about helping people to disentangle their lives from spiritual influences which, often unrecognized, have been blighting their lives. It engages the removing of hindrances to developing a deeper spiritual life and aims, to use a naval expression, to 'clear the decks for action.'

The difficulty is that many people, including Christians and their children, suffer from mental, emotional, moral and sometimes physical distress and have no idea that evil spirits are blighting their lives. This book helps to reveal ways in which Satan works. Then, two thousand years after Christ first fulfilled human hopes and began releasing men, women and children from demonic power, it shows how he still works in the same way. An attempt is made here to bring into perspective the profound simplicity of Jesus Christ's approach to the realm of supernatural evil as it affects people today. It suggests some ways by which a Christian may appropriate the victory of God's only Son over evil spiritual powers, right here and now.

I want to help dispel much ignorance and fear about spiritual matters which often still pervade the Church. Our adversary the devil must smirk when he can keep otherwise effective Christians at bay, befogged in misapprehension and nervousness. Yet the truth is glorious. A person of prayer and faith who does not trust in his or her own self, but in God through Christ, can treat evil spirits with fearlessness. Victory over them has been won by Jesus Christ through his Cross and Resurrection, and he wants us to share in it.

Many actual examples of deliverance from the powers of darkness, into the realm of Light and liberty, are included so that the practical principles of Scriptural truth can be seen in action. Every instance is factual; only the names of people or places have been changed to preserve confidentiality.

If Biblical understanding is 'pure theology,' then deliverance is one aspect of 'applied theology.' Deliverance ministry demonstrates the power of faith in Christ to exert spiritual 'purchase' upon the everyday world. The making free of those in spiritual bondage, or who are under demonic oppression, is not just the province of 'advanced' Christians. Far from it. It is entry-level Christianity. It was one of the first things Jesus taught his freshmen disciples to do.

'Deliver us from evil (Greek alternative, "the evil one")' is something for which Christians universally pray. The trouble is, often we have not understood the powerful grace with which Christ is ready to endow us to do the work so people can be delivered from evil. Doing the delivering that he and the Disciples did is still the business of the Church.

Jesus has not changed. However, in this area of faith often the Church has lost its fresh and jubilant experience. It is time we Christians took back the ground we have capitulated to a foe who has already been beaten, and whose power fades into insignificance beside that of the Lord and Master. Jesus readily equips his people for the work he has laid upon them, when they ask.

To stand before Christ on 'that great day', only to discover that we had within our grasp talents for deliverance which we never invested for the glory of God, would be devastating. For the help of countless demonically afflicted souls, I pray Christians will be strong and of good courage. Jesus our Lord shares with his people his victory, nothing less than the overcoming of the world, the flesh, and the devil.

I owe a debt of gratitude to the late evangelist, Edgar Trout, and the late Reverend Roy Jeremiah of the London Healing Mission (Anglican), who, in England, opened my eyes to things unseen. In North America, the late Reverend H.A. Maxwell Whyte provided encouragement when I needed it, and a lecture of the Reverend Derek Prince gave support. Dr Timothy Warner heartened me while I was working on a doctoral dissertation on seminary training for deliverance ministry. Unnamed others have shown by their writings that I have not been alone in this adventure for Christ and the relief of his afflicted children. Finally, I hope the many who have exhorted me to write on the topic, including Dr K. Neill Foster, will forgive me for having taken so long to get around to it.

Picton, Ontario

~ 1 ~

Surprised by Power

Divine Help for an Exhausted Minister

'It sounds like a demonic problem to me.' The man of late middle-age spoke quietly and with matter-of-fact conviction, as if he knew what he was talking about. It was 1966 and Michael Harper, a young writer and fellow priest in the Church of England, had recently introduced me to Edgar Trout. 'He can teach you something about the work of the Holy Spirit,' Michael had said. This was hard to swallow for one who had been trained at a prestigious English theological college. Could I learn something about spiritual life from a lay person of another denomination!? I soon found that to be with Edgar Trout was like being with one of the Apostles. When he prayed, one could almost feel the earth moving. Quickly I believed he had much indeed to teach me.

As the vicar of St Aidan's Ernesettle, a working-class city parish in Plymouth, Devon, two or three times I had seen people healed when I laid hands on them and prayed, or anointed them in the name of the Lord. I also knew Christians who never seemed to be able to find real joy in life, and people who had problems that no one seemed able to help. Psychiatrists and ministers, psychologists and surgeons had no answers for them. Some people had remorseless inner drives, uncontrollable thought-life, lusts or habits. Seemingly unconquerable moods forced individuals and their families to live under constant fear of the next bout of emotional oppression. Some of these were people of prayer and personal devotion. On my second meeting with Edgar, I found myself describing my feeling of helplessness over such problems. He responded to my tale of one person's woe with the extraordinary statement: 'It sounds like a demonic problem.' I could scarcely believe my ears!

My wife Delphine and I were completely committed Christians. We even believed in angels. In 1963 we had seen our five-year-old daughter Helen's life miraculously saved when she was bodily pushed out of the way of a falling stone chimney by an invisible being. I was happy to join with 'the angels and archangels, and all the company of heaven' in praise of God. But the notion that 'dark angels', evil spirits that Jesus had cast out of people in New Testament times, really existed to torment and trouble people had never been raised during my training for ministry. I thought 'having demons' was simply how people in olden times had described mental problems.

I soon found that Edgar took the Scriptures literally and practically. He and his immediate praying friends from many denominational backgrounds believed the word of God as it was written. They prayed accordingly, and then things happened. When I attended their prayer meetings, I found events to be utterly astonishing. People reported how Jesus Christ currently ministered with dynamic power to the needs of people. Edgar and his friends witnessed things that I thought had ceased with the closing of the New Testament. People experienced power and joy I had never believed to be possible in this world. Not only did they come into the experience of salvation, they were filled with the Holy Spirit as I had read about in the Acts of the Apostles.

One evening I heard a man who had been totally illiterate the previous week read the whole of the Authorized Version of Isaiah 53 with scarcely an error. It all seemed incredible, yet I had observed it with my own eyes. Sometimes members of this group mentioned 'casting out demons.' I listened with bated breath, hardly daring to believe that Jesus really still did today the same things that he had done during his days on earth: that Christians had the power to discern the activity of demons, and to cast them out in the name of the Lord Jesus Christ. With fast-beating heart, one day I prayed, 'Lord Jesus, if you want me to be involved in such a ministry, I am ready. It is totally outside my ability even to begin. I am full of ignorance and doubt if I could ever help folk as these people do. However, I put myself again in your hands. Use me to your honour and glory, however you want. Amen.'

Within a few weeks a lot happened. On a five-day silent retreat I made sure that all my known sins and sinful attitudes were confessed. I tried to muster a spirit of true repentance and humility. I knew I had been too busy with several ministry activities, along with being the sole priest of a busy parish. I was probably exhausted, though I would not have admitted it. I asked God to give me his direction and simplify my life. On returning home I went into what St John of the Cross called 'the dark night of the soul.' It was a period of deep separation from the intimacy of God. All I could do was fast and weep, and wonder. It was as if God was right beside me, but between us was a wall nine inches thick of clear, black glass. My wife Delphine and our four children knew something unusual was happening, and seemed to understand. For me it was a time that was both terrible and yet full of hope.

Shortly afterwards, a priest from the London Healing Mission, Roy Jeremiah came to preach and minister at St Aidan's church. While he was with us God healed me of a lung disease that the Canadian doctor had recently said would prevent me emigrating to Canada. At the same time, I experienced something of what the Bible describes as being *'filled with the Holy Spirit.'* I was a changed man. From temporary spiritual darkness I was delivered into a glorious light.

Within the next five days a letter arrived from the Canadian head office of the international accounting firm, Coopers and Lybrand, with whom I had worked before going to theological college. It offered me opportunity to move to Canada as a 'worker-priest.' There, like Paul the tent-maker who had worked in Corinth to support his preaching ministry, I would exercise my ministry while practising my old profession of chartered accountant. I chose to work in Canada's financial heart, Toronto.

Through Scripture and prophecy God told me to leave England by Epiphany (6 January 1967). It was now the end of November. To my amazement, my fellow clergy of the seven parishes of the North Plymouth Group were unanimous in their agreement. The Bishop of Exeter, Robert Mortimer, also added his confirmation. He immediately wrote, commending me to Bishop George Snell of Toronto. A few weeks later, Bishop Snell welcomed me personally and did everything he could to help me and my family settle in our new country. But before the Mitchell family and our cat and dog embarked on the Cunard Line's SS *Carinthia* something else that was to change my understanding about ministry took place.

~ 2 ~

Accompanying Signs[1]
Biblical Power in Practice Today

At two p.m. on 3 January 1967 I was alone in our stripped-down vicarage. Delphine and the children had departed from Plymouth by rail for Shakespeare's leafy county of Warwickshire to stay with my parents. We had sold almost all our furniture and belongings to raise funds for our family's great adventure. Toys, linens, Delphine's oak 'hope-chest,' my study chair, and an old heirloom grandfather clock, all the furniture we could bring, had to be crated in large wooden boxes and the lids screwed down.

I was working furiously, for the shipper's men were coming to pick up our crates at four p.m. The doorbell rang. A close neighbour stood on the step, the last person I would have expected to see. Mary was mother of a cheerful family, her husband George, and two grown up sons. Her dark curly hair crowned a face which was deeply wrinkled, making her look very much older than her forty-two years. I had first met her when I originally came to the parish in the street where she often walked, backwards and forwards, seemingly without any purpose. Then she had told me, 'I never go to my church. The only place I ever go is to my psychiatrist every month. I have terrible fears. I cannot enter the local store if anyone else is there. I wait outside until I will be the only customer, and then dart in quickly.' Mary told me of the crippling 'black pain' that would strike her belly at odd and frequent times. She had been seriously disabled by these symptoms since she was eighteen. Yet internists and surgeons could find nothing wrong with her.

Mary had seized all her courage to come to the vicarage to show my wife some photographs from her brother in Canada. But Delphine had gone. Despite the urgency of my work on the crates, I politely asked if she would show me her snaps. Inside, I wondered how quickly I could get rid of her. I needed every moment for screwing on those lids.

Finally, when she was on the front porch, leaving the house, for some reason I found myself asking, 'Oh, by the way, how are you keeping?' She answered, 'Still the same.' Now, to my utter astonishment I heard myself say, 'I know what is wrong with you. Satan has hold of you, and if you come back inside, God will heal you!' She looked as astounded as I felt, and wilted weakly against the wall. Wonderingly, I helped her back into the living room.

Questions about the onset of her problems sprang to my mind. Mary told me that, at the age of eighteen, she had gone to a medium who foretold that she would marry a foreigner. He would be a bad man, and her life would be cursed. In fact, she had married a foreigner, as many English women did during World War II, but he was a good man, and they had a strongly knit family. Mary had, however, indeed been cursed with the troubles that had afflicted ever since her visit to the medium. For twenty-four years she had experienced increasing fear in her life, and the pains had become a continuous plague to her.

I opened the truth of the Bible to Mary. She confessed to

God that by going to the medium she had disobeyed God's specific commands in Deuteronomy 18 and elsewhere. She asked forgiveness of that sin, and all others she could think of, and those she had forgotten. Mary wept as she knelt on the bare floor in the uncurtained vicarage living-room to commit her life to Jesus. She renounced the devil and every spirit of divination, and others related to the medium. Then I looked straight at her and commanded those spirits to leave. Mary spluttered, her eyes filled with tears and she said, with a smile of wonder, 'They've gone!' To my amazement, her face seemed to have changed. The lines on Mary's face had filled out. She looked years younger, and her voice had lost a characteristic flatness. Months later, in Canada, I received a letter from her saying her life had quite changed, and the 'black pain' was gone.

In Canada I soon began to find many people, both at church and in the businesses I visited in the course of my work as an auditor, who had demonic afflictions. The Lord had opened my eyes to see what I would not ordinarily have seen. I found I could understand spiritual causes behind many troubles affecting people's lives. Men and women began to find deliverance and salvation in a glorious way. I felt a wonderful liberty in my heart. The work of the ministry was suddenly lighter. I was discovering the truth that Paul experienced when he wrote to Timothy, '*God did not give us a spirit of timidity [cowardice], but a spirit of power, of love and self-discipline*' (2 Tim. 1:7). I felt that I would never again become a burned-out pastor, and somehow the terrible feeling of frustration I had felt with some people and about the condition of others would never return. I was right.

Notes

1. 'And these signs will accompany those who believe: In my name they will cast out demons; . . . ' (Mark 16:17).

Jesus *Is* Deliverance
The Model in Action

Jesus walked the length and breadth of the Holy Land and completely established the principles of liberty for humankind in three short years. He fulfilled all the prophecies and promises of God by teaching the truth, bringing people to repentance, and healing untold numbers of sick and demonized people. This was the love of God in action.

Jesus *is* Salvation. The New Testament word *salvation* also means *deliverance, preservation, safety.* The word sometimes translated into English as *to save* is also rendered *to heal, to make whole, to preserve, to rescue.* Jesus brought wholeness to the lives of men, women and children. In this work it was as important for him to cast out demons as it was for him to heal the sick and bring forgiveness to sinners. The Lord exercised a power over evil spirits that was fundamental to his salvation message.[1] The Jews had anticipated that the Messiah would cast out demons.[2]

Yet not all Jews thought like this. The powerful Sadducees of Christ's day believed in neither demons nor angels (Acts 23:8). Other people's ignorance, however, never stopped Jesus. He simply delivered people from the power of evil spirits as part of his saving work. Freeing men and women from the power of the devil was one of the chief characteristics of Jesus Christ's mission.[3]

In the first exciting days of his ministry Jesus returned to his hometown, Nazareth. There, in the synagogue one Sabbath, they brought him the scroll of Isaiah the prophet. He knew every word of the book which revealed the purpose for his whole life and death. So he quickly moved to the place where he read:

> *The Spirit of the Lord is upon me, because he has anointed me to preach good news to the poor. He has sent me to proclaim freedom for the prisoners and recovery of sight to the blind, to release the oppressed, to proclaim the year of the Lord's favour (Luke 4:18-19).*

Then he said, *'Today this scripture is fulfilled in your hearing.'* He was so forthright in this declaration of his Messiahship that the unbelieving, double-minded people, fellow citizens he had known all his life, wanted to throw him down the local cliff! When Jesus spoke, he was the actual embodiment of the Word of God he read from Isaiah, and that was altogether too much for his neighbours. It was as easy for them as it is for us to treasure the Bible and yet to oppose the practical reality of its message.

The 'prisoners' in need of freedom Jesus read about in Isaiah were not people in forged steel chains in the town jail. Their bonds were invisible, destructive emotions and habits. Their spiritual chains were mental and physical afflictions quite outside the normal realm of healing. Isaiah's 'oppressed' were not people who had bad landlords or bosses but those who *'were under the power of the devil'* (Acts 10:38).

Jesus fulfilled God's plan to inaugurate a new era of

freedom for the spiritually afflicted. He claims to be the one who himself 'ties up' Satan and plunders his kingdom of evil (Matt. 12:29). Why, he says, '*I will build my church, and the gates of Hades will not prevail against it*' (Matt. 16:18 NRSV). He goes further, giving power to the church, saying, '*I will give you the keys of the kingdom of heaven: whatever you bind on earth will be bound in heaven, and whatever you loose on earth will be loosed in heaven*' (Matt. 16:19). Gates are part of the defence of a fortress. Therefore Jesus is saying, 'No defence that Satan puts up can stand against my church.'

Yet the tragic facts of church history show that all too often Christians have been terrified of the defensive gates of Hades! Deere's words express the truth clearly: 'All fear of the devil is *irrational* fear. No Christian should ever fear Satan or any demon. The only person a Christian is taught to fear in the New Testament is God himself.'[4] Believers should recognize that behind the devil's vulnerable defences demons shudder! (James 2:19). Evil spirits know and tremble at the power that resides in the name of Jesus Christ and in his precious blood. They fear, with their master, the punishment in eternal fire which is prepared for them (Matt. 25:41). Once, as a woman was being set free from evil spirits, a demon said through her voice, 'Come on, we have to go. We can swim in fire!'

Immediately after the Holy Spirit had come down upon him at his baptism, Jesus was led by the Spirit into the wilderness '*to be tempted by the devil*' (Matt. 3:14-4:11). In the third temptation the devil, called by Jesus '*the prince of this world*' (John 12:31), showed Christ all the world's kingdoms and their splendour. '*All this I will give you,*' Satan said, '*if you will bow down and worship me.*' (Matt. 4:1-9).

The devil reeled from devastating blows as Christ, responding to each test with words from Scripture, brought the *'sword of the Spirit which is the word of God'* crashing down on him. Then the ruler of darkness retreated to lick his wounds *'until an opportune time'* (Luke 4:13). The coming of Christ into the human world meant absolute, overpowering condemnation of Satan (John 16:11). Yes, Jesus makes it clear, *'the prince of this world will be driven out'* (John 12:31).

The Lord's acts of deliverance were evidence that a far greater Prince had come. Jesus brought the kingdom of heaven into the world's present experience. Christ's mastery over the dominion of darkness (Col. 1:13) was a manifestation of the atoning power of the incarnate Son of God (Col. 1:15-23). This power focuses on the theme of Divine conflict and victory. Jesus 'fights against and triumphs over the evil powers of the world, the "tyrants" under which mankind is in bondage and suffering.'[5] Such power extends to Christ's followers who by faith, grace and the Holy Spirit share in his victory over the spiritual enemy of God and man (Mark 16:17).

Jesus knew that all who followed him would face temptations and afflictions from the devil. Therefore he taught his disciples to pray to the Father in heaven, *'Deliver us from the evil one'* (Matt. 6:13). Powerful, destructive forces of spiritual evil did not slow Jesus and his ministry down. Rather, they spurred him on to deal with them effectively both personally and through power delegated to the ordinary men whom he gathered around him. In his first act of commissioning Jesus gave his disciples specific *'authority to drive out evil spirits'* (Matt. 10:8; Mark 6:7). In Christ's mind, therefore, deliverance was basic, an elementary ministry fundamental to the Gospel. The Twelve took their commission seriously as shown by the results of their first experience of ministry when *'they drove out many demons'* (Mark 6:13).

Many believe the Lord showed that it was his intention that the practice of deliverance, a hallmark of his own ministry, should be practised by his followers throughout the ages.[6] Others, however, argue that only the Apostles could employ signs and wonders, such as exorcising evil spirits.[7] Yet, soon after commissioning the Twelve, Jesus sent out seventy-two others, less high-profile disciples, to prepare the way for him to visit selected towns and villages. These people, whose names we do not know, returned with joy to report to the Master what had happened: *'Lord, even the demons submit to us in your name,'* they cried (Luke 10:17).

Among the religious leaders were those who attributed Christ's power over demons to Satan. Our Lord called this unforgivable blasphemy against the Holy Spirit. Some even said, *'He is out of his mind,'* and Jesus' own family tried to stop him working. In response, Jesus actually substantiated his ministry to his family and the religious leaders upon the basis of his power and authority to cast out demons (Mark 3:20-28). This work was integral to the whole thrust of the Gospel.[8] Jesus sums the matter up, *'If I drive out demons by the Spirit of God, the kingdom of God has come upon you!'* (Matt. 12:28).

Some of the people set free from demons by Christ may already have become followers. For example, the woman Jesus delivered from eighteen years of bondage by a crippling spirit appears to have been a faithful believer, *'a daughter of Abraham'*[9] (Luke 13:10-16; Rom. 4:11,16; Gal. 3:7). Mary Magdalene also may have been a member of the fellowship for some time when she was delivered from seven spirits (Luke 8:2).

Christ recognized that warfare with the forces of Satan would continue after his departure from earth. In the parable of the weeds he says the *'sons of the evil one'* will attempt to overcome the *'sons of the kingdom'* until *'the end of the age'* (Matt. 13:38-39). In what is thought by some scholars to represent part of the very early church's summary of Christ's teaching,[10] Jesus promises that deliverance will continue, *'And these signs will accompany those who believe: In my name they will drive out demons; . . .'* (Mark 16:17).

Shortly after he said these words, on the Feast of Pentecost, the Holy Spirit came suddenly upon about a hundred and twenty gathered and expectant men and women. He brought gifts of power so disciples could bear witness to Jesus *'to the ends of the earth'* (Acts 2:8). Paul understood how to use this power in his personal ministry and considered it more effective even than his preaching (1 Cor. 2:4-5). He saw the continuing need for human deliverance from Satanic bondage, first taught and demonstrated by the Lord.

The constant demonic struggle for the control of human lives is shown by the Philippian slave-girl who had *'a spirit by which she predicted the future'* (Acts 16:16-18). Paul, fulfilling Mark 16:17,[11] commanded the spirit out of her *'in the name of Jesus Christ.'* Her powers of divination immediately left her. This manifestation of the Holy Spirit's authority angered her masters who had profited from her fortune-telling ability. The success of this woman's deliverance quickly led to Paul and his companion, Silas, being severely flogged and thrown into prison.

The fearless Apostle exhorted Christians in Ephesus to *'Put on the full armour of God so that you can take your stand against the devil's schemes'* (Eph. 6:11). He made his reasons clear: *'For our struggle is not against flesh and blood, but against the rulers, against the authorities, against the powers of this dark world and against the spiritual forces of evil in the heavenly realms'* (Eph. 6:12). *The weapons we fight with are not the weapons of the world. On the contrary, they have divine power to demolish strongholds'* (2 Cor. 10:3-4).

Christ, Paul says, *'disarmed the powers and authorities and made a public spectacle of them, triumphing over them by the cross'* (Col. 2:15). The victory of Jesus Christ (the Anointed One) is the basis of the church's power over evil spirits because Christians (the anointed) have received *'fullness in Christ, who is the head over every power and authority'* (Col. 2:10).

Paul charges Christians to remember that part of our spiritual inheritance involves knowing God's 'incomparably great power' (Eph. 1:1-19a). The use of the verb 'to know' here has the sense of 'know how' or 'to be skilled in', implying the practical use of this power. This great power, explains Paul, compares with that 'mighty strength' with which the Father raised Christ from the dead and brought him into heaven (Eph. 1:19-20). God, in his 'manifold wisdom', commissions his church to make plain Christ's 'unsearchable riches' to the whole gamut of the powers of darkness, and so to manifest the eternal purpose of God (Eph. 3:10,11).

Besides Paul, other New Testament writers face the reality of human conflict with demonic powers. The records of Christ's and the disciples' deliverance ministry are contained in the Synoptic Gospels, Matthew, Mark and Luke. John provides other perspectives. He pithily describes Christ's purpose in the ongoing war between God and Satan: *'The reason the Son of God appeared was to destroy the devil's work'* (1 John 3:5-9).

When Jesus says, *'Everyone who sins is a slave to sin . . . is in bondage to the devil'*, John reveals a view like Paul's. John records the saying of Christ, *'If the Son sets you free, you will be free indeed'* (John 8:36). To those who rejected his message Jesus says, *'You are unable to hear what I say. You belong to your father, the devil. . . . He is a liar and the father of lies'* (John 8:31-47). John's focus is upon the crux of Christ's whole ministry of redemption. The cross, rather than exorcism, marks the defeat of Satan and his league. The cross is God's instrument for the adversary's utter downfall and rout (John 12:31; 14:30; 16:11). The glorious news is Jesus the crucified, risen and ascended Lord brings life and makes people whole.

James, 'the brother of the Lord,' understands how the devil works on human minds. The enemy digs and capitalizes on natural weaknesses to gain a hold over people. The Apostle observes that the devious human heart is able to generate a certain kind of wisdom which is 'of the devil' (James 3:15). Disobedient believers must recognize they have desires which 'battle within' (James 4:1). James calls on them to correct their attitudes and motives. *'Submit yourselves to God,'* he commands, *'Resist the devil, and he will flee from you'* (James 4:7). A simple, fearless practicality in dealing with supernatural evil is James' hallmark.

Simon Peter, in his first letter, urges his readers to *'be self-controlled and alert'* for their *'enemy the devil prowls around like a roaring lion looking for someone to devour.'* Peter continues, *'Resist him, standing firm in the faith. . . .'* (1 Peter 5:8-9). Satan's work is many-faced, employing spiritual forces of evil which can affect multitudinous areas of life. But he can be combatted victoriously.

The eventual outcome of the battle between the forces of the Kingdom of God and the dominion of darkness is portrayed in Revelation, the Bible's last book. Satan will be *'thrown into the lake of burning sulphur'* (Rev. 20:10). Before that great day the Christians will overcome Satan *'by the blood of the Lamb and by the word of their testimony'* (Rev. 12:11). No matter what suffering the devil may inflict, Christians will vanquish him. Their faith will be in the power of the blood of Christ to win them total liberation from the devil's work. This will be true although, meanwhile, the devil causes the earth great trouble; he *'is filled with fury, because he knows that his time is short'* (Rev. 12:12).

Thus the New Testament, from the Gospels to Revelation, testifies that deliverance is a hallmark of Christ's personal ministry. It is integral to his work of salvation. The Apostles Paul, Peter, John and James say that the Christian life involves a spiritual battle against the devil's influences. The realities of this demonic sway, and the Christian's part in breaking it, are often mentioned.

According to the New Testament, the word of God and power of the Holy Spirit are available for Christians to overcome and root out demon influence. The Lord shows that he intends his followers to practise deliverance. Christ wants this ministry to continue throughout the ages, along with preaching and healing, and every aspect of the ministry he inaugurated. This is what he means as, on his last night, he says: *'I tell you the truth, anyone who has faith in me will do what I have been doing. He will do even greater things than these, because I am going to the Father'* (John 14:12). What a promise this is for believers to embrace today! Victory over Satan and his influence has come through the person of Jesus Christ and the Cross. Jesus *is* deliverance.

Notes

1. Warner, Timothy M., *Spiritual Warfare: Victory Over the Powers of This Dark World* (Wheaton, IL: Crossway Books, 1991), 36.
2. McCasland, S. Vernon, *By the Finger of God* (New York: Macmillan, 1951), 136.
3. Crehan, J.H., 'Exorcism in the New Testament'. In Dom Robert Pettitpierre, ed., *Exorcism: The Report of a Commission Convened by the Bishop of Exeter* (London: SPCK, 1972), 11.
4. Deere, Jack, *Surprised by the Power of the Holy Spirit* (Grand Rapids: Zondervan 1993), 97.
5. Aulen, Gustav, *Christus Victor: An Historical Study of the Three Main Types of the Idea of the Atonement* (London: SPCK, 1931), 4.
6. Among those who have written that deliverance is meant for the church of today are:
- Anderson, Neil T., *The Bondage Breaker* (Eugene: Harvest House, 1990).
- Bubeck, Mark I., *The Adversary: The Christian Versus Demon Activity* (Chicago: Moody, 1975); *Overcoming the Adversary: Warfare Praying Against Demon Activity* (Chicago: Moody, 1984); *The Satanic Revival* (San Bernardino: Here's Life, 1991).
- Burnett, David, *Unearthly Powers: A Christian Perspective on Primal and Folk Religion* (Eastbourne, Sussex; MARC, 1988).
- Foster, K. Neill, *Warfare Weapons*. Camp Hill, PA: Christian Publications, 1995).
- Friesen, James G., *Uncovering the Mystery of MPD* (San Bernardino: Here's Life, 1991).
- Horrobin, Peter, *Healing Through Deliverance: The*

Biblical Basis (Chichester, England: Sovereign World, 1991).

- Kraft, Charles, *Defeating Dark Angels: Breaking Demonic Oppression in a Believer's Life* (Ann Arbor: Servant Publications, 1992).
- Murphy, Ed., *The Handbook for Spiritual Warfare* (Nashville: Nelson, 1992).
- Unger, Merrill F., *What Demons Can Do to Saints* (Chicago: Moody, 1991).
- Wagner, Peter & F. Douglas Pennoyer, eds., *Wrestling with Dark Angels* (Ventura, CA: Regal Books, 1990).
- Warner, Timothy M., *op.cit.*
- White, Thomas B., *The Believer's Guide to Spiritual Warfare*. Ann Arbor: Servant publications, 1990).
- Whyte, H.A. Maxwell, *Dominion Over Demons*. 3rd edn. (Toronto: H.A. Maxwell Whyte, n.d.).
- Wimber, John, 'Power Evangelism: Definitions and Directions'. In *Wrestling With Dark Angels*, C. Peter Wagner and F. Douglas Pennoyer, eds. (Ventura: Regal Books, 1990).

7. Lane, William L., *The Gospel of Mark*. The New International Commentary on the New Testament (Grand Rapids: Eerdmans, 1974), 207.

8. Finger, Thomas N. and Willard M. Swartley, 'Deliverance and Bondage: Biblical and Theological Perspectives'. In *Essays on Spiritual Bondage and Deliverance*, ed. Willard M. Swartley. Occasional Papers No. 11 (Elkhart: Institute of Mennonite Studies, 1988), 27.

9. Unger, Merrill F. *op. cit.*, 101.

10. Rawlinson, A.E.J., *The Gospel According to St Mark*, Westminster Commentaries (London: Methuen, 1925), 247.

11. McClung, L. Grant, 'Pentecostal/Charismatic Understanding of Exorcism'. In *Wrestling with Dark Angels*, C. Peter Wagner and F. Douglas Pennoyer, eds. (Ventura: Regal Books, 1990), 209.

~ 4 ~

Nothing New Under the Sun
Deliverance down the Centuries

'Signs and wonders' often accompanied the work of the early church as recorded in the book of Acts. Today, many Christians sense the reality of demonic activity and also the power which God graciously gives to the church for dealing with evil spirits. Believers are rediscovering that they have Holy Spirit authority. The church is learning anew what our brothers and sisters of the early Christian centuries took as a matter of course. Spiritual warfare demonstrated by acts of deliverance from demonic bondage were then all in a day's work. Today, front-line ministers are again learning the essentials of this long forgotten, but fundamental element in Christ's saving work.

Writings of the church Fathers from the end of the Apostolic age through the next four hundred years contain many examples of people dealing with evil spirits. Descriptions of healing and deliverance were part of the normal Christian experience. Demons were treated seriously, for example, by St Justin Martyr (c. 100 – c. 165). Justin places God's purpose to save human beings on a level with his determination to devastate evil spirits. He says Jesus was made man 'according to the will of God the Father for the sake of believing men and for the destruction of demons.' As

21

a result, Justin asserts, 'Many Christian men have exorcized in the name of Jesus Christ ... numberless demoniacs throughout the world ... they have healed them, and still do heal, rendering the demons impotent and driving them out.'[1]

Living in the second and early third century after Christ the great Tertullian claimed that the Christian power of exorcism was well-known and undeniable. 'All the power we have over them is from our naming the name of Christ, and recalling to their memory the woes with which God threatens them at the hands of Christ as Judge. ...'[2]

During the first three centuries, when exorcism was considered to be a ministry grace which all Christians possessed, the church did not rely on professional clergy. Every Christian could exercise general Christian power and authority, which included exorcism.[3] Exorcism was not on the fringe of ministry for early Christians but 'an important part of their mission.'[4] Believers not only recognized the existence of the demonic realm, they treated demons as afflicting powers of the enemy which were to be exorcized triumphantly in the name of Jesus.[5]

Not only in their streets, homes and assemblies, but wherever the church existed the domain of evil spirits was recognized and their power challenged by Christians. For example, the Desert Fathers, including Antony of Egypt and the Palestinian Hilarion, dealt with the expulsion of demons as a normal element in their ministry.[6]

From earliest times catechumens, those coming from paganism into the Church, were required to be delivered as part of their preparation for baptism.[7] The church did not have to prove these folk were raving maniacs, it was sufficient that, as a consequence of original sin and personal sin in the case of adults, they were more or less subject to the power of the devil. This meant they had to renounce the 'works' or 'pomps' of the devil 'from those whose dominion the grace of baptism was about to deliver them.'[8] Nobody, including those born of Christian parents, could be without demons, Optatus thought, and they had to be driven out before coming to the font.[9]

For nearly four centuries the ministry of deliverance had been exercised by 'rank and file' Christians. During the period which followed the legalizing of Christianity by Emperor Constantine in AD 312, the legislative weight of Rome began to embrace the administration of the church. The Council of Carthage (AD 398) prescribed the rite of ordination for exorcists, but this did not forbid others from practising exorcism.

The modern penchant for some people to distinguish theoretically 'good' demons from the 'bad,' as, for example, supporters of 'white' witchcraft versus the 'black' kind, would have been recognized in the days of Augustine (c. 354-430). He emphatically denied that the 'so-called good demons are to be courted.'[10] Augustine developed in some detail his notion of conflict with evil spirits in *The Christian Combat*.[11]

Conflict with evil spirits continues to figure in Christian ministry down the years. In medieval times dynamic Bernard of Clairvaux (1090–1153) had a reputation for a powerful ministry which drew many people to him for exorcism.[12] A hundred years later a contemporary of the holy Francis of Assisi (1181/2–1226) says 'many men and women, tortured by divers torments of devils ... were delivered' by Francis.[13]

That the church had authority over the powers of darkness was never in doubt. The power of Christians indwelt by the Holy Spirit was all that was needed to enable the church to meet Satanic forces victoriously. Thomas Aquinas (1225–74), for example, considered the church indestructible under the temptations of demons and undermining attacks of the devil.[14] To him, most human problems and difficulties stemmed from evil spirits while it fell to the angels of God to communicate God's revelation to people.[15] He believed that people are taught to understand from the Incarnation that the author of evil does not rank above humanity, nor should people be cowed by the devil.[16]

Aquinas said that while demons attack people by inciting them to sin, they may also be sent by God to attack a person for the purposes of punishment and drive the sufferer to God. God's grace and the guardianship of angels are humanity's compensation.[17] The devil's aim is to find out about the interior state of the person, the better to tempt him with a vice to which he is more prone and so dispose his will in a certain way.[18] To do this, demonic power is directed to manipulate the human mind: 'Demons can effect a change in a man's imagination and even in his bodily senses, so that something appears to be other than it is. ...'[19]

From the earliest days we can see that Christians were convinced, with Christ, that humans are in spiritual conflict with Satan and his demonic forces. They were equally certain that Christ had won victory over the powers of darkness. Both in their personal experience and in their teaching they emphasized that Christians have the power to obtain deliverance from demons in the name of Jesus Christ. This perception of the spiritual battle continued through the Middle Ages.

The reality of spiritual conflict as a theme emphasized by many writers persisted into the Reformation period. Martin Luther's (1483–1546) great hymn, *A Mighty Fortress Is Our*

God, is a monument to that Reformer's understanding of the
spiritual battle:

> For still our ancient foe,
>   Doth seek to work us woe;
> His craft and power are great,
>   And, armed with cruel hate,
>   On earth is not his equal.

Humans, however, have the 'right Man on our side . . . and
He must win the battle.' (*Hymns of the Christian Life, No
11*).

People who like to think that demons are figments of the
imagination will find the great Reformer John Calvin
(1509–64) a powerful opponent. He argued against those
'who babble of devils as nothing else than evil emotions.'[20]
Calvin supplied texts which emphasized the reality of human
conflict with the devil and demons.

> The fact that the devil is everywhere called God's
> adversary and ours ought to fire us to an unceasing
> struggle against him. For, if we have God's glory at heart,
> as we should have, we ought with all our strength
> contend with him who is trying to extinguish it.[21]

Calvin recognized the supreme reality that neither the devil
nor any of his demonic host can operate beyond the will of
God, who allows them to afflict believers.

> So he governs their activity that they exercise believers
> in combat, ambush them, invade their peace, beset them
> in combat, and also often weary them, rout them, terrify

them, and sometimes wound them; yet they never vanquish or crush them. But the wicked they subdue and drag away; they exercise power over their minds and bodies, and misuse them as if they were slaves for every shameful act. As far as believers are concerned, because they are disquieted by enemies of this sort, they heed these exhortations: *'Give no place to the devil'* (Eph. 4:27, Vg.). *'The devil your enemy goes about as a roaring lion, seeking someone to devour; resist him, be firm in your faith'* (1 Pet. 5:8-9a), and the like.[22]

The Reformer shows how the Old and New Testament saints David and Paul were not free from this sort of strife. It is 'common to all the children of God.' Because, in Christ our Head, victory always fully existed, there is liberty in Jesus which will be made perfectly complete when 'we shall have put off our flesh.'[23]

The man who brought the fire of revival to eighteenth century England, John Wesley (1703–91) claimed that evil spirits, while they may 'transform themselves into angels of light,' are also to be found 'about our bed, and about our path.' They 'spy out all our ways,' seeking whom they may beguile with subtlety. Wesley explained, with detailed examples, that it is Satan's work to strive to instil passions which are contrary to the fruit of the Spirit, continually inciting men to evil.[24]

While history shows that the Biblical perspective of the existence of the evil spirit world continued down through the centuries, the Reformation marked a change of attitude towards deliverance ministry. Though the church still recognized the reality of spiritual warfare within human life and character formation, the practice of exorcism fell noticeably into disuse, particularly amongst Protestants for whom the concept was negatively influenced by Luther and Calvin.[25]

Notes

1. Justin Martyr, St. 2 *Apology* Chap 6. Quoted in *The Ante-Nicene Fathers: Translations of the Fathers down to 325.* Edited by Alexander Roberts and James Donaldson. American Reprint of Edinburgh ed. (Grand Rapids: Eerdmans, 1953), Vol. 1, 190.
2. Tertullian. Apology 23. *To Scapula*, quoted in Michael Green, *Evangelism in the Early Church* (London: Hodder and Stoughton, 1970, reprint, Crowborough, Sussex: Highland, 1984), 231.
3. Vagaggini, Cyprian, *Theological Dimensions of the Liturgy: A General Treatise on the Theology of the Liturgy*, translated by Leonard J. Doyle and W.A. Jurgens from the 4th Italian ed. (Collegeville, MN: Liturgical Press), 426.
4. Twelftree, Graham, *Christ Triumphant: Exorcism Then and Now* (London: Hodder & Stoughton, 1985), 133.
5. Green, Michael, *Evangelism in the Early Church* (London: Hodder & Stoughton, 1970, reprint, Crowborough, England: Highland, 1985), 148.
6. Green, *op. cit.* 148, quoted in John Wimber with Kevin Springer, *Power Evangelism: Signs and Wonders Today* (London: Hodder & Stoughton, 1985), 153.
7. Kelly, Henry Ansgar, *The Devil at Baptism: Ritual, Theology and Drama* (Ithaca: Cornell University Press, 1985), *passim.*
8. Toner, Patrick J., 'Exorcism and the Catholic Faith', quoted in *Exorcism Through the Ages*, St Elmo Nauman, ed. (New York: Philosophical Library, 1974), 37.

9. Optatus, n.d. *Donatir IV*, c. p.75, quoted in Edmund B. Keller, 'Glimpses of Exorcism in Religion', in *Exorcism Through the Ages*, St Elmo Nauman, ed. (New York: Philosophical Library, 1974), 286.

10. Augustine of Hippo, Saint, *City of God*, n.d., David Knowles, ed. (Harmondsworth, England: Penguin, 1972), 344.

11. Augustine of Hippo, Saint, *Christian Instruction*, translated by John J. Gavigan; *Admonition and Grace*, translated by John Courtney Murray; *The Christian Combat*, translated by Robert P. Russell; *Faith Hope and Charity*, translated by Bernard M. Peebles, quoted in *The Fathers of the Church: A New Translation*, ed. dir. Roy Joseph Deferrari (Washington: Catholic University of America Press, 1950), Vol. 2, 315-22.

12. Bernard of Clairvaux, Saint, *Acta Sanctorum*, n.d. Augusti, Vol. 4, 106, quoted in Edmund B. Keller, 1974 'Glimpses of Exorcism in Religion,' which is quoted in *Exorcism Through the Ages*, St. Elmo Nauman, ed. (New York: Philosophical Library, 1974), 267.

13. Brother Thomas of Celano, *Vita Prima et Secunda S. Francisci Assisiensis*, Rome, cap. III. 'De Demoniacis', 1880, Rom. ed. 1906, 142. Translated by A.G. Reffers Howell, in *The Lives of St. Francis* (London, 1908), quoted by Edmund B. Keller in 'Glimpses of Exorcism in Religion,' which is quoted in *Exorcism Through the Ages*, St. Elmo Nauman, ed. (New York: Philosophical Library, 1974), 271.

14. Aquinas, Saint Thomas, *Theological Texts*, selected and translated by Thomas Gilby (London: Oxford University Press, 1955), 342.

15. Kelsey, Morton, *Discernment: A Study in Ecstasy and Evil* (New York: Paulist Press, 1978), 70.

16. ibid., 278.

17. Aquinas, Saint Thomas, 'The World Order,' in *Summa Theologiae*, n.d., Vol 15. 1a 110-19, translated by M.J. Charlesworth (London: Blackfriars, 1970), 75.

18. ibid., 79.

19. ibid., 85.

20. Calvin, John, *Institutes of the Christian Religion*, Book I, Ch XIV, edited by John T. McNeill (Philadelphia: The Westminster Press, 1960), 178.

21. ibid., 174.

22. ibid., 176.

23. ibid., 176-7.

24. Wesley, John, *The Works of John Wesley*, editor in chief, Frank Baker, Vol. 3, Bicentennial edition (Nashville, Abingdon Press, 1986), 24.

25. King, Paul L., 'The Restoration of the Doctrine of Binding and Loosing', in *Alliance Academic Review 1997* (Camp Hill, PA: Christian Publications, 1997) 61-2.

~ 5 ~

A World View Worth Watching
A Modern Mind – Set in an Eternal Frame

(G)od and the realm of angels, with Satan and his demons, provide the spiritual background, the framework against which men and women and children live out their lives. Their lives are, in turn, not only physical lives in a material world, but spiritual ones. In every human heart there is a 'nostalgia' for heaven and a reality that is far greater than all we presently see. Every human being has a sense of the numinous, of the transcendent and righteous Creator.

For the practitioner of 'primal religion', the animist, every occurrence is fraught with spiritual meaning. The universe is open with a blurred line between natural and supernatural. The material world integrates with the realm of gods and spirits.[1] The crops are sown and marriages consummated when times are propitious and the spirits have been pacified. In the ancient and basic human religion people look for causes in the supernatural as well as in the natural realm.

Western culture trains us to search for meaning only in the sphere of measurable and 'scientific' nature. We have been educated to forget our background and, as a result, many have lost our spiritual orientation. How did this happen? To answer we must look back a long way, to the disturbing days of the fourteen hundreds.

The first stirring of the great spiritual revolution we know as the Reformation began over five hundred years ago. Irreversible changes in the whole arena of western thought were beginning. Renaissance Christian Europe was becoming a restless sea of lay and religious ideas. The scene was being set for the Reformation which, in the sixteenth century, would lead to a significant shift in the spiritual world view of much of the church.

By 'world view' we mean that mental framework which gives shape to our existence. Our world view integrates our knowledge and understanding of this world, our perceptions about human life, about moral social realities, and about our reason for existence. For Christians, as for humankind naturally, the realm of spiritual good and evil is part of their world view.

With the sixteenth century new, radical, theological and social thought took shape. From the ranks and leadership of the church, which had previously been united under the medieval power of the Pope, rose men like Luther, Calvin and Knox. They and their followers rejected the corruption and worldliness of the Holy See. Though Rome responded with the Counter-Reformation and revival of piety, a time of great turmoil set in. Every part of western Christianity was affected. Reverberations from those confusing and innovative times are felt to this day. One small but important element of Reformation turmoil concerned the way in which churchmen thought about exorcism.

Long part of the church's armoury, deliverance ministry had become mainly limited to liturgical exorcisms of adult and infant candidates for baptism. Some Reformers may have considered it to be merely a needless popish ritual, for they treated exorcism with extreme caution. Though exorcism remained within some of the new liturgies, such as the 1549 Book of Common Prayer which emerged from this turbulent period, this was not without many a bitter disagreement.

In England, Bucer's strong disparagement of any kind of exorcism led to its removal from the baptismal rite of the Second Prayer Book of 1552. By 1604, the Canon 72 of the Church of England specifically forbade any minister to practise exorcism 'without licence or direction ... of the Bishop' under threat of severe punishment and 'deposition from the ministry.'[2] John Darrell, of St Mary's in Nottingham (Church of England) was tried in 1598 and, though never sentenced, imprisoned under Canon 72.[3]

In contrast, within the Roman Catholic church exorcism continued. Ignatius Loyola (1491 or 1495-1556), the founder of the Jesuits, was particularly aware of the spirit world. In his autobiography he emphasised the need for spiritual discernment. But the Reformers were strongly influenced by the Renaissance's newly found humanism. This was an enhanced view of the centrality of mankind in the created scheme of things. It embraced an attitude of mind which credited utmost significance to humanity's 'faculties, affairs, temporal aspirations and well-being.'

Hitherto, the medieval church's concept was that a man's life on earth was significant only because it bore on the mercy and grace of God after his death. Renaissance man perceived this view as belittling to humanity. Humanists 'asserted the intrinsic value of man's life before death and the greatness of his potentialities.' The swing towards the significance of humanity restored some balance to pre-Reformation excesses. However, this benefit was offset by a deflection from the Biblical view of the significance of the spirit world.

The shift in western attitudes concerning the work of Satan

emerged more fully with the philosophical movements in the seventeenth and eighteenth centuries.[4] Many religious leaders began to develop a rationalism which, with social, political, and economic factors, led ultimately to a denial of the supernatural power of both good and evil.

This rationalistic world view, along with other influences, has greatly affected the theology of the western church.[5] Harvey Cox represented a widely held theological position. In *The Secular City* he said that the New Testament exorcisms simply represent the powerful effect of the culture of the times, along with organic and social components. Jesus, by his exorcisms, was dealing with people's 'neurotic constrictions,' Cox says, and 'projected fantasies.'[6] For others also, the notion of 'evil spirits' is seen mainly in cultural terms. Some assert that behind the pre-scientific images represented by demons and spirits is the reality of a warped and twisted human ego.

So, from the Reformation to modern times, the church has numbered in its ranks thinkers for whom exorcism in traditional terms was a reality. However, this view has not been held universally, and the trend, until the mid-twentieth century, has been away from the long-established biblical world view.

The biblical world view recognizes three realms:
1. The Realm of God.
2. The Realm of Angels.
3. The Realm of People and Things.

Briefly stated, the traditional world view perceives the Almighty living and reigning from a realm of glory which is invisible: *'No one has seen God and lived.'* The work and realm of angels is intermediate between God and the earthly realm of human kind. Their presence and ministry is referred to repeatedly throughout the Bible, from Genesis to the Revelation. While they live and fulfil a large part of what exists in the presence of God – *'Let all God's angels worship him!'* (Deut. 32:43) – they also have a ministry to the earth and people. *'Are not all angels ministering spirits sent to serve those who will inherit salvation?'* (Heb. 1:14).

When God has wanted to communicate directly to human beings he has often used the appearance of an angel to accomplish his purpose. In the Old Testament 'Christophanies' occurred, the pre-incarnate Christ himself appearing as *'the angel of the Lord.'* He gave instructions from the throne of God. He came to Hagar in the desert (Gen. 16:7-13). He called to Abraham twice from heaven, to prevent the sacrifice of Isaac and to bless his offspring (Gen. 22:11-18). He accompanied Moses and Israel's army in the wilderness (Exod. 14:19).

Whenever God wanted to intervene in the affairs of people in a way that required conversation, he did so angelically. Both Balaam, on his journey to bless Israel's enemies by cursing Israel, and his tormented donkey, were confronted by the Angel of the Lord with his drawn sword (Num. 22:22-25). The Angel of the Lord on another occasion, identifying himself as God the giver of the Covenant, appeared to the Israelites at Bokim and sharply rebuked them (Judg. 2:1-6).

In addition to the Divine Angel, angelic creatures, from Michael and Gabriel to *'men clothed in white,'* appear to God's people in Old Testament and New Testament times. Jacob dreamt of *'a stairway resting on the earth, with its top reaching to heaven, and the angels of God were ascending and descending on it. There above it stood the LORD. ...'* (Gen. 28:12-13). This angelic occasion marked a profound change in Jacob the shepherd's life as a similar dream affected

Joseph the carpenter centuries later: *'An angel of the Lord appeared to him in a dream and said, "Joseph son of David, do not be afraid to take Mary home as your wife, because what she has conceived in her is from the Holy Spirit. ..."'* (Matt. 1:20).

Again and again angels appear to key figures in the redemption story. They announced the birth of Christ to the humble shepherds. At the end of his life Jesus knew in the Garden of Gethsemane that he had only to call on his Father and he would *'at once'* put at his disposal *'more than twelve legions of angels'* (Matt. 26:53).

Angels were always mysterious and mythical to me in my early days as a minister. In those days an elderly clergyman spoke to me critically of Sir Basil Spence's modern angels depicted on the huge glass doors of the post-war reconstructed Coventry Cathedral. 'Who's ever seen an angel like that?' he asked. My reply was, 'Who has ever seen an angel?' Well, I have learned a lot since then. I have met people who have seen angels and been able to describe their appearance and relay their words. I have seen an angel at work, though he remained invisible. It happened like this.

Our daughter Helen was five years old. Delphine and I, with our four young children, were on a post-Easter holiday in the English county of Gloucestershire. We had met Delphine's mother, who had been born near the town we were visiting. She stopped to speak to a person she had known years earlier. While we stood waiting for her Helen drifted away, under my watchful eye, onto the vacant parking lot of an ancient Cotswold stone-built inn.

As I watched her, Helen was suddenly shoved invisibly from behind, her head and arms flying backwards. She ran up to cling to my leg. 'Helen, what happened?' 'Daddy, someone pushed me!' she said, her eyes big with amazement. Just then, a huge stone top of the inn's centuries-old chimney crashed down to the very spot where Helen a few seconds before had been standing.

Every sceptical grain in my soul was swept out in that moment. I knew what I had seen with my own eyes. As a family we gathered in a shop doorway and gave thanks to God. 'Thank you, Lord Jesus, for your great love and for the angel you sent to save Helen.' We all sensed something very profound had happened in the invisible world of the spirit to give the dramatic earthly result. I wondered if Helen had some special role one day to play in the family of God.

She grew safely through childhood to be successful in scholastics and sport, became a teacher, married the man God had prepared for her, became a mother of three children and today plays a significant role in the church. Yes, I believe in angels! But my question was, 'How did the angel know to push Helen? Had her guardian angel seen a "dark angel" from Satan's side pushing on the chimney to destroy that little child?' Somehow, I think so.

This is not as ridiculous a notion as one might think. Demons are painted with the colours of their master, the devil. Did not Satan himself face Christ in the wilderness and include the temptation to jump from the highest point of the Jerusalem temple? Satan's minions are called by Scripture demons, unclean or evil spirits whose work is to wreak destruction and death, to spoil God's Creation and thwart his design. But they can never win the ultimate victory, though in individuals and nations they may win skirmishes.

To explain the inexplicable, the perceived but invisible interference and mischief people experience, secular folklore produced goblins, imps and leprechauns. These, in western culture, are the mythical remnants of a time when the people believed that the affairs of men and women were influenced by the supernatural, both bad and good. Even during the Second World War pilots and aircrew in the Royal Air Force credited 'gremlins' with causing the malfunction of equipment such as motors, instruments and machine guns.

The interference and frightening behaviour of ghosts and poltergeists are recorded in every culture. Their reality has been recorded in a whole range of ways, from ancient stories, through personal records, to modern psychic research. Though a blessed sense of humour has allowed humans to call their more minor malign interferences 'mischief,' these spiritual forces are bent on evil. There exists a realm of angelic activity that is the polar opposite of the gracious ministry of the angels of God.

Within every human child born on earth there exists an intuitive sense that life is not limited to what we see. Human nature includes a sense of the supernatural. It has an intuition that God is good and that he blesses the affairs of people. Alongside this perception may be found an instinct that other, less well-intentioned spiritual forces exist whose purpose is to violate the good of human beings.

The signs are that western culture cannot remain much longer satisfied with a secular-materialist-humanist world view. Such is the fundamental human need for spiritual meaning that in the hardened, intellectual and materialistic western nations the 'New Age movement' has emerged. This may be seen as a sensitive, even if misguided, yearning to provide an ambience and a world view where spiritual reality can be discussed and believed in.

Any balanced Biblical world view, however, must acknowledge that Jesus Christ spent a considerable part of his ministry dealing with evil spirits which afflicted the people of his time. If Christians are to address the world effectively, if they are to match Godly teaching with Godly manifestations of healing and delivering power, they must have the *'mind of Christ'* and see things through his eyes. Can any other be a truly Christian world view?

Notes
1. Burnett, David, *Unearthly Powers: A Christian Perspective on Primal and Folk Religion* (Marc: Eastbourne, 1988), 19.
2. Summers, Montague, *The History of Witchcraft and Demonology* (London: Routledge & Kegan Paul, 1926), 231.
3. Richert, Corinne Holt, *The Case of John Darrell, Minister and Exorcist* (Gainsville, FL: University of Florida Press, 1962), 1, quoted in *Exorcism Through the Ages*, St Elmo Nauman, ed. (New York: Philosophical Library, 1974), 282-3.
4. Brown, Colin, *Miracles and the Critical Mind* (Grand Rapids: Eerdmans, 1984), 23.
5. Schaeffer, Francis, *The God Who Is There* (London: Hodder & Stoughton, 1968), 175-6; Hiebert, Paul G., 'The Flaw of the Excluded Middle,' *Missiology*, 10 (January 1982), 35-47; Warner, Timothy M. *Spiritual Warfare: Victory Over The Powers of This Dark World* (Wheaton: Crossway, 1991), 23-32 – among others.
6. Cox, Harvey, *The Secular City*, revised edition (New York: Macmillan, 1965), 131-4.

~ 6 ~

Reborn of the Holy Spirit

God's Grace to Overcome the Power of Evil

'**M**ay God himself, the God of peace, sanctify you through and through. May your whole spirit, soul and body be kept blameless at the coming of our Lord Jesus Christ' (1 Thess. 5:23).

Paul's beautiful blessing is upon people in the tripartite nature of their life – spirit, soul and body. A human being is both a single person and a unique unity of the three rudiments of spirit, soul and body.

Christians use the term 'Holy Trinity' to describe the mystery revealed to us as the One true God who is Father, Son and Holy Spirit – 'Three-in-One.' At the apex of his creation God made humanity, in some way, a reflection of the Holy Trinity. A single human person is also a mystery comprising three elements, the physical, the mental and the breath of life – body, soul and spirit.

Scripture reveals the magnificent truth that people are created in God's image: *'So God created man in his own image, in the image of God he created him; male and female he created them'* (Gen. 1:27). The image of God is most clearly reflected in the human spirit, for *'God is Spirit,'* Jesus said (John 4:24).

The first book of the Bible pictures the creation of Adam,

his body, spirit and soul, in these words: *'And the Lord God formed man from the dust of the ground [body] and breathed into his nostrils the breath of life [spirit], and man became a living being [soul]'* (Gen. 2:7). We can envision a person's God-given spirit bringing life from heaven to the seed of father and mother at the moment of conception.

From such a miraculous instant the baby's physical body begins its nine-month journey to completeness and birth. God says to Jeremiah, *'Before you were formed in the womb, I knew you'* (Jer. 1:5). The psalmist speaks of the Creator's point of view as he beheld the formation of the psalmist's unborn frame: *'When I was woven together . . . your eyes saw my unformed body [Hebrew, "embryo"]'* (Ps. 139:15). More than physical growth continues in the womb during the exciting months of pregnancy. The eternal spirit begins the shaping of the new human's eternal mind/soul. A person's character begins forming right from the start.

Every excited first-time parent knows immediately that their newborn child is a 'self,' a he or she with a unique persona. In the earliest days after birth the distinct personality and unique mind of the child begin to show. No two mind/souls are ever the same. Even when twins are identical in so many ways, their souls are unique: they are, without doubt, distinctive persons. The problem is, every child is also a natural-born sinner! God's whole desire for each child is the reformation of his or her soul until it is clearly becoming Christ-like, and fit for heaven.

When someone dies the eternal elements, spirit and soul, leave this earth to return to God: *'[His] dust returns to the ground it came from, and [his] spirit returns to God who gave it'* (Eccl. 12:7). At the Moment of his death, Jesus called out with a loud voice, *'Father, into your hands I commit my spirit'* (Luke 23:46). Holy Stephen, first martyr for Christ, as he was being stoned, prayed, *'Lord Jesus, receive my spirit'* (Acts 7:59). We shall all *'die once, and after that, . . . face judgment'* (Heb. 9:27). When we die, our spirit with its integrated, life-formed soul/character stands before Christ.

Jesus made the way to heaven clear both by his example and by his words, the most fundamental of all being those he spoke to Nicodemus: *'I tell you the truth, unless a man is born again, he cannot see the kingdom of God.'* Then, by way of explanation, he added: *'Flesh gives birth to flesh, but the Spirit gives birth to spirit'* (John 3:3,6). When a person believes in Jesus, it is the human spirit that is reborn by the grace of God and power of the Holy Spirit.

At salvation the believer's body is not reborn, neither is his soul reborn, though it is mightily changed by its new direction towards God. Now, it is not only generated by its human spirit, but regenerated by the Holy Spirit. From the moment of initial salvation the soul/mind has a new purpose. From being self-centred it has become God-centred.

The working out of one's salvation (Phil. 2:12) sees the Christian's natural mind being replaced by *'the mind of Christ'* (1 Cor. 2:16). In other words, the soul/mind's conversion has experienced a changing mode and quality of life. This is the work of the Holy Spirit. God's grace is cooperating with the loving and obedient soul. Christians increasingly think and act like Christ because his gracious Spirit enables them. This is the transformation *'into his likeness with ever increasing glory which comes from the Lord, who is Spirit'* (2 Cor. 3:18).

Satan, conversely, hates both God and God's creation, especially humankind, which is most dear to the Creator.

Whatever the devil can attempt to spite God and his purposes, he will. He wants to 'dis-grace' the Lord's people.

God allows Satan enough latitude to test us, and so sharpen our character, but the Lord always gives his children sufficient grace to keep them safe. He provides grace so that we may overcome all temptations: *'And God is faithful, he will not let you be tempted beyond what you can bear. But when you are tempted, he will also provide a way out so that you can stand up under it'* (1 Cor. 10:13).

The devil began his operations against the human race at the first opportunity, with Adam and Eve in the Garden of Eden. He continues to apply his energies to frustrating God's purpose and spoiling his handiwork. The resurrection of Christ and the destruction of the power of death it announced sounded the ultimate defeat of Satan and his dark angels. They know they are condemned, and their time is short. Therefore they are bent upon as much evil as possible, while they have time, to thwart the desires of the Holy One.

Evil spirits therefore attack, harass and oppress human individuals with the aim of capturing their minds/souls. They want to affect people's bodies, and influence their deeds for evil so that they will fall under God's judgment. Satan wants to take as many to hell with him as he can. To that end he and his forces wage an unceasing battle against the minds/souls of men, women and children everywhere, and will use people as instruments whenever they can. Jesus said, *'Woe to the world because of the things that cause people to sin! Such things must come, but woe to the man through whom they come'* (Matt. 18:6-7).

The devil incites men, women and children to rebel against God and all that is good, and to serve the cause of self and sin. Demonic powers lust to corrupt people in their imagination. John Wesley once warned that it is easier for the devil to put a picture into the mind of a man than it is for one man to whisper into the ear of another. The enemy wants to devour humans by playing upon their natural appetites and needs. Every existing situation and relationship, every potentiality can be his target. The evil-one is, simultaneously, both gross and obvious (to discerning Christians) and subtly clever in his battle for human souls.

This is the original spiritual conflict which began in the Garden of Eden and will continue until the return of Christ. Meanwhile, 'We have the right man on our side,' as Luther's hymn melodiously puts it, Christ himself. He will never leave us or forsake us. In constant faithfulness, from moment to moment, he gives gracious comfort, encouragement, strength and spiritual authority to those who have been reborn by the Holy Spirit.

~ 7 ~

Uncovering Demons

Learn to Recognize Evil Spirit Activity

A person's spiritual rebirth means that he has entered an entirely new and intimate relationship with the Almighty God. When I receive Jesus Christ as Lord and Saviour, I become nothing less than a Child of God (John 1:12) and his heir, a co-heir with Christ (Rom. 8:17).

Salvation is a startling and glorious event. Indeed, the only way to describe it is to say, *'everything has become new.'* This amazing beginning marks initiation into a revolutionary way of life with God. He is at the centre and Christ is in the heart. Such a radical reorientation of my perspective and reason for living will result in the progressive purification and strengthening of my Christian character. By the power of the Spirit I experience the miraculous advance in my character growth and experience. The only way to describe it is to say that I am moving 'from glory to glory.'

God's purpose is nothing less than the incarnation of Christ in each human life. The Christian should advance to a time of total self-offering to God when he calls upon the Lord Jesus to baptize (fill) him or her with the Holy Spirit. Christ has not changed; he knows that Christians today have as much need to be filled with the Spirit as did the men and women of the Jerusalem church (Acts 1 & 2). He wants his followers to bear powerful witness to him all over the world, beginning at home. Once baptized, believers should continue to pray daily to be filled with the Spirit so that the process of spiritual growth and development, along with power for service, may continue as long as they live (Acts 4:29-31).

The experience of being baptized in the Holy Spirit often brings hitherto hidden demons to the surface where they can be recognized and dealt with. When a person is as fully committed to Christ and as truly open to his Spirit as possible, and prays to be filled with the Holy Spirit, the fresh bubbling of the Spirit floods into the person's whole life. Any spiritual darkness becomes more clearly observed and felt. Because such elements are now quite insufferable and hateful, the Christian looks for relief. Deliverance is the Christ-given answer.

It is not rare for faithful, believing people at any stage of their life in Christ, to find that one or more distressing symptoms of the old life remain, and may be more conspicuous than before. Certainly, Christians are more conscious of them than in the old days. Some aspects of living simply do not seem to respond to their heartfelt repentance and confession of sin. They feel trapped by a habit, attitude or frame of mind that will not respond to earnest prayer. Sometimes they wonder if they have really ever been saved; are they truly in a state of grace? How could they really be Christians when they continue to be racked by anxiety or paralysing fear? Perhaps it is a dread of death, sickness or poverty. How could they be truly reborn children of God when they feel so bad? For example, they may remain emotionally cast in a character-mould of rigidity or pride. They might experience an uncontrollable urge to manipulate or control others, or suffer from seething anger that can boil over into rage. An imagination that roams wild into realms of sexual, violent or bizarre fantasy could be causing their distress. Rampaging sexual, gluttonous desires, or habits that drive them relentlessly every day, seem insurmountable. Apprehension about their true state will dominate their mind when it seems to them that they are governed by attitudes and behaviour they have learned to hate.

Spiritually oppressed people often present themselves to their minister or priest, to their elders and prayer groups for intercession, but nothing seems to work. They remain blocked in, bound and helpless to obtain the victory which they are sure, from his word, Christ wants them to have. They do not realise that they are struggling with spiritual forces. They are in the clutch of demons.

They have now to discover the glorious liberty brought by Jesus that Peter describes to the Roman centurion Cornelius and his family and friends:

How God anointed Jesus of Nazareth with the Holy Spirit and power, and how he went around doing good and healing all who were under the power of the devil, because God was with him (Acts 10:38).

'Being under the power of' the devil is from the original Greek word *katadunasteuo,* 'to exercise harsh control over one, to use one's power against one.' Two translations render it 'oppressed by' the devil (KJV and NASB). This expresses the evil will of the devil who wants 'to lie heavy upon, weigh down the spirits, imagination, govern tyrannically . . .' This is how our English word 'oppress' is defined in the Concise Oxford Dictionary.

We know that demons often cause devastating and

demoralising thought and behaviour patterns such as those described. In many hundreds of cases simple deliverance ministry has dealt with the difficulty, and the problem has forthwith disappeared! 'The proof of the pudding is in the eating!'

A natural question, often posed, is *'How can demons affect real Christians like this?'* My personal experience with many people over thirty years has led to this response: they almost inevitably 'picked up' their demons before they exercised true, obedient faith in Jesus Christ. I say this is usually true because committed Christians will almost never expose themselves to fresh demonization. They joyfully intend to lead the new life, and they have the presence of Christ within to stimulate their conscience and give them victory over temptation. But it can happen. Christians can get caught!

A strong Christian leader visiting India was taken out for a special 'late-night treat' by his Hindu host. Exhausted after a busy day, the Christian would rather have gone to bed. He was unprepared physically, emotionally and spiritually for the 'treat.' It turned out to be a visit to a Hindu temple in the height of a festive season. He returned soon after to Canada. Only after six months of intense depression was it discerned that this was demonic oppression dating from the heathen temple visit. He was speedily and instantly delivered after appropriate prayer.[1]

You might ask, *'Why are all people not delivered from demonic affliction when they become Christians?'* Maybe some, or most, do indeed experience instant deliverance from some or all evil spirits when they are spiritually reborn. There is no way of telling. I do know this, however, that countless faithful people, long after they first receive Christ into their lives, continue to be subject to demonic interference. Their subsequent deliverance is manifest and beautiful, when dealt with appropriately.

Demonic manifestations in the bodies and on the countenances of some people undergoing deliverance, and their words, seem to indicate that evil spirits can remain in a Christian's body. The question often raised is, '*How can a demon reside in a person whose body is a temple of the Holy Spirit?*' (1 Cor. 6:19). Is it really possible for the evil spirit to dwell in the presence of the Spirit of Jesus? Well, yes, I think it is.

Look at it like this. Christians universally believe certain essentials about the nature of God: the Lord is (i) omniscient [knows all there is to know]; (ii) omnipotent [all-powerful, the Almighty], and (iii) omnipresent [everywhere]. As the Psalmist says to God,

If I go up to the heavens, you are there; if I make my bed in the depths, you are there. If I rise on the wings of the dawn, if I settle on the far side of the sea, even there your hand will guide me, your right hand will hold me fast. . . . For you created my inmost being; you knit me together in my mother's womb (Ps. 139: 8,9,13).

There is no place and no state of existence in Creation where God is not present as the all-seeing, sustaining power (Heb. 1:3). Indeed, it has been truly said 'even the devil is God's devil.' The evil one can do nothing unless permitted to do so under the sovereign will of God (Job 1). The point is, the devil exists in the presence of God and the demons also exist in God's universe, where he is everywhere, by his permission. It is not difficult, therefore, to see that evil spirits can remain within yet imperfect humans after they have come to know Christ.

To illustrate: We have seen in the previous chapter that when a person is reborn of the Holy Spirit, the *spirit* is reborn; the *soul/mind* is not reborn but is changed in its direction, neither is the *body* reborn but it begins a new existence under the control of a Christian personality.

A key part of the work of evil spirits is to conquer a person's will, to usurp the grace of God in a human soul. Their purpose is to control or manipulate the human mind and affect behaviour for the worse. It matters not whether they do that from within a person's body, or from outside it, they can still have their effect.

Merely being brought up in the church and having a general belief in Christ should not be presumed sufficient to change a person's quality of life so that he or she is 'demon-proof.' Once demons find a way open for them they will fasten themselves upon, or invade, their victim. Often, even though for periods apparently dormant in their distress and terror at finding their 'host' has become a true Christian, they remain until they are commanded to leave.

We now need to consider what actually are the circumstances that can open up 'space' for demonic invasion. Three common means of access that demons have to a person's life seem to be these: (i) personal sin, (ii) inheritance from previous generations, and (iii) close contact with demonized people or places.

Note
1. The visit to the Hindu temple occurred at the end of a very tiring day and the Christian leader had no idea where his host was taking him. It was at a special festival time and the place was full of people and the incense of their idol

worship. He was immediately swept up into a frame of mind that was *'intrigued and curious.'* Then he found that *'his heart was becoming fearful.'* The Christian had to confess that he had opened his mind to the full effect of the idol's presence and the spirits of the idolatrous worshippers. This meant wholehearted repentance and renunciation of every spirit to which he had exposed himself on that occasion.

A Christian may enter with impunity any place where evil spirits are present providing the intention and attitude of the heart are right. First, one must only enter after prayer to the Lord to ensure, as far as possible, that it is not against his will. Then, the Christian *should advance as if in warfare order* against the powers of darkness there: this means going in the Name of Jesus and under the power of his Precious Blood. It requires a person to banish mere curiosity and openness to anything other than facts as they are observed. One's intention on entering the realm of the wicked one should be for the purpose of immediate confrontation with the evil there, even if silent, or to equip oneself better for the future battle with the adversary on behalf of God's afflicted 'little ones.'

~ 8 ~

The Commandments – Handle with Care!

Mock God's Authority, and Pay the Consequences

Habitual or violent breaking of any of the Ten Command-ments (Exod. 20), or other moral laws of God (e.g., Lev. 18 and 19) may lead directly to demonization. People who consistently break the moral commandments of God expose themselves to the powers of darkness. They open their souls and bodies to the personal affliction of spiritual beings. These are demons which, until now, have tempted and pressured them towards the sins of the flesh. They tempt everyone, as Christ also was tempted (Luke 4:13). It is in yielding to these temptations consistently, or in moments of great crisis, that the dark spirits are given a dangerous 'space' in a human life.

Now, *'All have sinned and fall short of the glory of God'* (Rom. 3:23). Does this mean that everyone is demonized? No! It does not. We are all 'tarred with the same brush,' the inheritance and propensity for disobedience that comes from our disobedient forebears, Adam and Eve. Christ came to give liberty from the grip our sinful human nature has on us. He gives to all who believe in him a spiritual life renewed from the inside out. This is God's gracious gift, a gift which no one can earn by good behaviour. *No amount of determination to keep morally upright, or success in obeying the Commandments, can redeem us.* Only personal acceptance of the efficacy of Christ's self-sacrifice and shed blood can do that (Heb. 9; Rom. 3:24-25, etc.).

We agree with Paul that every person alive is guilty, to some extent at least, of breaking the Laws of God. Further, this for most people is without ever accumulating evil spirits. It appears, however, that when a person becomes *committed* to some way of wickedness, he or she may open his or her life to direct, personal demonic invasion or powerful, sustained oppression.

The level of commitment to sin which reduces a person to such a point may differ from one individual to the next. Any continuous, wilful practice that is offensive to God may suggest such a danger.

Picture demons as Satanic creatures hell-bent on pressing against the good in human nature. They rely upon the natural human propensity for self-pleasing. Imagine evil spirits as creatures playing upon the strings of a human heart, causing a resonance with evil leading to sinful agreement. Bad thoughts, words and deeds result, for which the soul is guilty. ('The devil made me do it,' is no excuse. Every individual bears the responsibility for his decisions.) Demons aim to drag people down into rebellion against God's love and righteousness. They seem to penetrate a person's character.

Such demons, which reside around or within someone, *might* gain access from a one-time involvement with wickedness, especially the occult realm. Involvement usually means wilful interest, but we have known demonic affliction to fall upon the innocent. For example, a child's happy ritual for years, daily on returning from school, was to visit the 'dear old lady' who lived two doors down the road for homemade cookies and pop. She had no protection from the spirits that infested the woman's welcoming house. The woman was a professional medium.

Consider the following examples of people whose rebellious way of life and breaking of Commandments opened them up to demonic interference. Their lives dramatically changed for God's glory through deliverance ministry.

Destruction in the Tongue

In everyday life we frequently offend God without 'picking up' a demon. For example, consider the third commandment: *'You shall not misuse the name of the Lord your God, for the Lord will not hold anyone guiltless who misuses his name'* (Exod. 20:7). The words of Jesus support this: *'... men will have to give account on the day of judgment for every careless word they have spoken'* (Matt: 12:36). God takes very seriously the way we use our tongues. Picture the amateur carpenter letting out a curse when he hits his thumb with his hammer! He is probably just showing that he has a little more sanctification to come, not that he has a demon!

But the man or woman whose language is habitually profane, vile and full of expletives is different. He could be under the influence of spirits committed to human destruction. Let us give them a capital letter and call them by the names of the afflictions which drive and seemingly control the behaviour of a person. We will call them Cursing, Swearing, Evil-Speaking and Blasphemy.

Johnny, a young man successful in business, made a heartfelt act of repentance and became a Christian at the tragic funeral of his drunken friend, Mike. Johnny wanted baptism so much, but found that, though his approach to life had undergone a radical change, he was unable to control his tongue. He had prayed much about this and had become so depressed with his vile language that he thought there was no way he could be baptized. Upon further repentance and confession of his sinful habit and renunciation of the above named spirits, we commanded them out of his life. Johnny felt immediate release; his face lit up with joy. He experienced complete deliverance from the problem which had been with him for years, and he was soon happily baptized.

Was the genuine repentance and confession all this young man needed? Apparently not. He had done that often. The experiential release came upon renunciation and exorcism of the specific demons related to the breaking of the third commandment: 'You shall not misuse the name of the Lord your God' (Exod. 20:7).

Deadly Adultery

The seventh commandment is, 'You shall not commit adultery' (Exod. 20:14). Adultery means sexual intercourse by a married person with someone who is not his or her spouse. The holiness of God, however, is such that any kind of illicit sex affronts him.

Marriage between a man and a woman is the divinely ordered relationship within which sexual fulfilment is part of the purpose of God. It is the only proper and godly relationship within which he approves physical sexual expression. Satan will do anything he can to inflame human passions so that people become involved in sexual relations outside marriage. Such behaviour exposes individuals to the possibility of demonization. This, in turn, can lead to a sexual life that veers into excessive, gross, indecent, uncontrollable ways.

Often people have reported their behaviour has got so out of hand that they despair of ever being normal again.

They simply can neither control their lust nor manage their actions.

The boy or girl who gives in to the natural sexual impulse or peer-pressure and then engages in fornication (sex outside of marriage) may not immediately pick up a spirit, Fornication. However, if 'sleeping around' becomes a style of life, then such a demon could gain access. The young person would have no idea what had occurred because he or she is a habitual fornicator anyway.

Only after coming to know Jesus Christ does the youngster, perhaps now a man or woman long grown up, realise that powerful inward pressures toward sexual sin remain that simply will not submit to repentance, earnest discipleship, prayer or intercession. In such circumstances deliverance can afford an immediate and glorious experience of the liberty that is in Jesus.

As a prosperous businessman, Shawn had many affairs. The day came when he allowed his wife to take him with her to church. Not long afterwards, he received Christ as Lord and Saviour and, in a Pentecostal setting, received a glorious infilling of the Holy Spirit. Several months after he had begun this new life he appeared on my doorstep in great alarm. He had just committed adultery, completely against his desire and new-found belief in Jesus. He told me his story.

After becoming a Christian he had avoided business-oriented social gatherings. Often in the past they had provided opportunities for sexual liaisons. A few nights earlier he had decided the time had come for him to take advantage of a wine-and-cheese party to spread the Gospel to business acquaintances. As he entered, he saw a woman he had never met before looking at him from across the room. Instantly, the idea flashed through his mind that he would have sex with her before the night was out! He dismissed the thought, determined to remain true to Christ and to his wife, and circulated among the people. Later, he was introduced to the woman and, hating himself all the way, to his shame found himself in bed with her. What had happened?

I suggested this explanation of the episode: 'Shawn, the spirit of lust that had such a riotous time in your life in the old days, since you became a Christian has kept a low profile, waiting for you to slip up. You went to the wine and cheese party without prayer, determined, in your own strength, to do some witnessing for Christ. You entered that room outside the will of God. As you entered, the spirit of lust in you recognized the spirit of lust in the woman across the room. That was the source of the feeling that came to you. In that instant the deal was made between the demons. They would strive to ruin you both. The evil in you both drew you together.'

We took the necessary steps for deliverance. When I saw him again, after many years, he gave glory to God that he had never had another moral relapse. What happened to Shawn is not uncommon. The man had become a Christian after accepting the Cross of Christ. The power of the blood of Jesus, crucified and raised from the dead, had brought him into new life. Like many coming to Jesus, he had not realised the depths of his sin. There had been no renunciation of the devil. Dormant spirits remained in him to surge up at an opportune moment to take him unawares.

The divorced organist of an evangelical church choked as she confessed to her repeated adultery with the handsome and lustful husband of her friend in the same congregation. She was desperately attached to the man, but was also under the conviction of the Holy Spirit that she must be free of him. She had prayed and willed to be able to resist his inevitable advances. However hard she tried, in the event she would always succumb to them. She hated herself for what she was doing, for hurting her friend, for causing her Lord grief and putting her own soul in jeopardy.

She was delivered from lust and adultery while kneeling in prayer. At her renunciation of the spirits and the command for them to leave, she went through a sudden, violent orgasm and was rid of her problem from that time on.

All sexual sins are related to adultery because they spoil the God-ordained sanctity of human physical and mental sexuality. Michael was a divinity student about to complete a postgraduate degree and go into full-time ministry. He was devout, sincere, committed to world evangelism, and a man of prayer. Michael had a problem that has become increasingly common among Christians in recent decades. He was addicted to looking at filthy books, and with this masturbation which always appears in tandem with pornography.

Michael had an excellent record not only as a student but also as a practising minister. He was a happily married family man. Shamefacedly, he described a recent event to me:

'I have confessed and repented countless times over the years. I have promised God that I would not even enter a place where they sold sex books. Just last week, as I was walking, I saw a bookstall and was determined not to go in. As I was passing, it was as if I had a hook in my nose. It pulled me into the place and, before I could stop myself, I had bought some more books. I hate myself for this compulsion. I seem powerless to overcome it.'

Michael's childhood home had been over the family's corner-store where his father had sold pornography 'under the counter.' His parents were not Christian and their son had never been taught the self-discipline of the 'custody of the eyes.' Sneaking into the shop during the night at a young age Michael had become addicted to pornography's attraction, and to masturbation as a result.

Now I led him into an act of repentance that went right back to his earliest experience with the forbidden material. He asked God to forgive him for stealing magazines as a child. He acknowledged that his father was a sinner too, in engaging in a trade that offended God. Michael confessed that he had a deep resentment against his dad for having the books on the premises, leading to Michael's downfall.

When I was satisfied that Michael had brought every aspect of his addiction to the feet of Christ, he received assurance of the Lord's forgiveness. He renounced every spirit of pornography and masturbation. I agreed with him and confirmed that all evil spirits affecting him must go. I looked Michael in the eye and said, 'Michael, I am looking at you, but I am not speaking to you. Evil spirits, Michael is a child of God and you have no right to him. In the Name of the Lord Jesus Christ, go from this man. Go to the place prepared for you!' Michael sat bolt upright and said, 'They're gone! I felt them leave! Oh, hallelujah!'

Subsequent enquiry satisfied me that he had indeed entered a life of liberty from that time on. There were psychological elements in Michael's case, as there are in every troubled life. However, nothing in any psychological therapy that I have ever encountered could have provided such instant and complete relief from severe moral disorder. Michael, especially since engaging in his studies for the Christian ministry, had thrown his heart into 'classical' treatment of his bondage to sin. He was totally committed to evangelism, discipleship and personal growth, yet only the deliverance steps led him into lasting liberty. Now he enjoyed, for the first time in his life, 'a good conscience towards God.'

'You Shall Not Steal' (Exod. 20:15).
Mary Jane had been in a provincial psychiatric hospital for eighteen years. While on a rare two-day pass she visited me. Her problems stemmed from an infatuation with a man much older. She had become a kleptomaniac. When I met her she was quite heavily under the influence of prescribed drugs.

Discovering the root of her personal distress many years earlier was simple. Next, Mary Jane needed to understand the infinite value she had as a person God had loved from her conception. This love was far greater than any affection a man could ever give her. She accepted the truth of the Gospel, repented of her sins, renounced the thieving spirit, and was delivered.

Within a few weeks her stay at the 'psych' had terminated and she returned to the town she had left in deep distress so many years earlier. She maintained her new walk in the company of Christ. Not long after release Mary Jane went through a short period when, every time she went out, she insisted on buying things she could not afford. This was not demonic but a reaction to having freedom and a little money after having been institutionalized for half of her life.

'You Shall Not Murder' (Exod. 20:13).
Murder is a sin which is so serious that it carries a high risk of demonization. It can also come under many guises. Jesus said that anger could merit judgment under the sixth Commandment (Matt. 5:22). Apparently lesser violent emotions such as hatred, bitterness and resentment are also related. Abortion is another word for murder. Women, or

men who have advocated their girlfriend's abortion, almost always confess it as 'murder.'

A woman came to see me who had been unable to bear a child since she had married, though she had conceived and miscarried eight times. I asked her about her morals before and since marriage. Jennifer confessed that she had been promiscuous before her conversion to Christ. Twice she had conceived and she had procured surgical abortions on both occasions.

This Christian woman's heart was broken as she told me her story. She had confessed the abortions as the sin of murder when she became a believer, but had never felt forgiven even though she believed the biblical truth about God's willingness to forgive any sin, save the unpardonable one. She mourned deeply for her two aborted children. Jennifer once again, for the last time, laid her sin at the foot of the Cross. She renounced the devil and the spirits of murder and abortion. The words of deliverance manifestly set her free. Shortly afterwards she conceived and brought forth a healthy daughter. The spirit that had caused her to abort spontaneously eight times, was gone for good.

'You Shall Have No Other Gods' (Exod. 20:3).
Say the words of the first Commandment to a North American and, unless the listener is an immigrant from an eastern country where there are many gods, he might easily say, 'Who ever heard of anyone worshipping an idol?' Yet there are many people who remain in spiritual darkness because they shut out the light of Christ by their idolatry.

The kind of sin we are considering here is not what might popularly be thought idolatrous. No doubt there are people for whom the most important element in life, before any thought of the Almighty, is their golf game, money, work, car, clothes, vacation cottage, education, hobby, wife or husband. *Anything* can be a 'god' if it is more important than one's relationship with Jesus Christ and the Heavenly Father. But there is a class of sin under this Commandment that involves the worship of other spirit beings, demons. Dabbling in the forbidden realm of the occult is all too common in the western world.

The Bible condemns idolatry outright again and again. Moses gave the following warning from God to his people:

'Let no one be found among you who ... practices divination or sorcery, interprets omens, engages in witchcraft, or casts spells, or who is a medium or spiritist or who consults the dead. Anyone who does these things is detestable to the LORD' (Deut. 18:10-12).

In the Old Testament the Jews constantly fell from grace. The perennial afflictions born by the Jews over many centuries all stemmed from their failure to remain faithful to the One true God.

Even in the New Testament John warns his readers, *'Dear children, keep yourself from idols'* (1 John 5:21). Worshipping the material objects fabricated by craftsmen in human or animal likeness as gods was bad enough. Much more serious was the fact that these objects drew people into the worship of demons (Lev. 17:7; Deut. 32:17; Ps. 106:36-7; Rev. 9:20). Paul explained it like this: *'The sacrifices of pagans are offered to demons, not to God'* (1 Cor. 10:20).

The devil can be imagined as mocking God every time a person bows down towards a material object in worship. He will jeer at Christ because he knows that every act of idolatry is the worship of one of his demons, sent to the idol to draw the human heart right away from the Lord of heaven and earth. The spiritual force behind the idol is powerful and effective in blinding the mind and giving spurious spiritual satisfaction to the soul.

I discovered the power of idols one day in the city of Bombay, India. I had visited heathen temples and viewed the lonely worshippers and their hideous man-made gods. It was beyond me why any man or woman could actually believe these things were worthy of worship. Then I stopped before a grimy shop window full of Hindu idols for sale. As I looked at a row of dusty elephant-gods, voluptuously and femininely cast in cheap pink plastic, carelessly painted, I prayed in my heart with sympathy for the poor people who believed in such things. 'How, dear Lord, can anyone actually *worship* these things?'

The Lord's answer was immediate. For a period of about ten seconds I felt an immense sexual yearning and welling up for those hideous fabrications. God let me experience a demonic force behind the god. I quickly called out, 'Right, Lord, I see,' and the sickening feeling left me as quickly as it had come. But what a powerful effect the experience had! God had granted me insight into the power that inhabited a pagan idol, a power that is supernatural and perverse, striking at the unreasoning heart of human desire.

People from the western world may not worship man-made gods like those of the eastern religions, but they are often caught up in idolatry, nevertheless. Not only 'toys,' cars, boats, places in the country, or even wealth are worshipped. Think of those for whom the world of the occult, fortune-telling and astrology have a fascination. To human curiosity about the future, we now turn.

~ 9 ~

Deadly Curiosity

Dangers of the Occult: Counterfeit Spiritual Gifts

The word 'occult' means 'secret.' Holy Scripture, of course, gives instruction about how we are to deal with the occult. *'The secret things belong to the LORD our God, but the things revealed belong to us and to our children forever, . . . '* (Deut. 29:29). People seeking to break into the secrets of the future, or past, are attracted to ouija boards, astrology, fortune-tellers of all kinds, New Age 'channelers' and spirit mediums. The unknown future has an especially strong attraction. Girls want to know about their romantic future, wives look for hope in troubled marriages, and women in difficult 'relationships' want to know if there is any hope.

Males of the species are not free from curiosity, either. In 1969 I attended a high-power meeting of venture capitalists in the city of Toronto. The advertised speaker began by crediting his success in finding profitable investments to a spirit-guide. When, from my place at the back of the crowd, I saw what was happening, I decided that no evil spirit was going to get glory that day!

The speaker was so bold that he proposed to display spirit-guidance at work before the eyes of the sophisticated crowd. This suggestion caused a flurry of whispers among the keenly interested professionals from the heart of Canadian business,

Toronto's Bay Street. They had been drawn to the meeting by the speaker's much publicised success.

I began immediately to pray silently and powerfully in the spirit, with amazing results. Nothing worked for the man! The speaker was baffled and embarrassingly disconcerted when the spirit failed to communicate with him. His obvious disquiet caused a ripple through the high-priced audience. Collectively it shook its head, muttered, smiled, and began to leave. What a farce! Hallelujah! Our God reigns, *everywhere*, including in the land of the Bay Street barons!

The future belongs to the Lord our God, and if we want to know about the future, we can ask *him*. The future is nonexistent at any moment in time: it always lies within the provenance of God. Since it has no physical actuality, existing only in the mind of the Creator, the future is spiritual. It has not yet become part of our history, is not material, real, tenable. God did not design the future to be known, controlled, or in any way manipulated spiritually by human beings.

To ask God about the future is an act of *worship* of the Creator, a spiritual exercise which is worthy of him alone. He may choose to answer our questions about days to come, but normally he will not.

Life in Christ is a life of faith and trust. God requires his children to believe that he knows every detail about their needs, and that he will supply them. All they must do is give their top priority to seeking his will (Matt. 6:33). He knows that the main reason people want to know the future is for profit. The desire to feel such godlike power is what ruined Adam and Eve. Christians believe that God has told us, through the Biblical revelation of his purposes, all that is vital about the future.

When someone asks a ouija board to tell him about the future he is not asking a board-game, an upturned glass or a pointer. He is asking a spiritual question of the evil spirit 'behind' the ouija board. The person who solicits help from a fortune-teller is, in reality, seeking advice from the spirit of divination or familiar spirit that uses the fortune-teller as its agent. In other words, he is *worshipping* the demon. This is plain, old-fashioned, heathen idolatry.

Such acts of submission and subservience to evil spirits put innumerable people into servitude and spiritual bondage to that and, potentially, other demons. This is why God forbids us to indulge in curiosity about the unknown, why such practices are 'detestable' to him. Scripture shows that to be detested by God is to be under the sentence of death.

God's design for human beings is that we should so agree with him that we discover the reality of *life in all its fullness*. It was to give humankind this quality of life that Jesus came into the world (John 10:10). Human self-interest and ambition inspire occult meddling which is hateful to God, who is not happy to have to punish sinners in order to bring them back on track. He hates the occult because people involved in its dark practices confound his glorious purpose for them. God's best possible blessing can only be accomplished when humans obey the laws of Divine love.

No sin is more effective than idolatry in causing a break in relationship between God and people. Worship directed towards any 'not-God' proves that an individual is moving away from the Sovereign Lord on a polar-opposite bearing. Idolatry cuts us off from blessing and will erase our name from the divine Book of Life.

A nest of spirits can infest the life of an occult practitioner or frequent dabbler. It includes demons which work through tarot cards, teacup-reading, numerology, pendulums, palmistry, séances, astrology and any vehicle that supernaturally investigates the unknown. Once an occult spirit has gained access, there is a risk that it will attract other demons. 'Fear' would be a prime candidate for acceptance, as in the case of Charlie, a middle-aged man who had immigrated from England in his early days.

Nervous and unsure of himself, Charlie and his wife came under the influence of his mother who was enthralled with fortune-telling. He remembered the night when, sitting around the kitchen table in the old family home, the ouija board session had turned into a nightmare of activity. It spelled out things that were totally unknown except to one person there. A fear had gripped Charlie and seriously affected his life for the next thirty years in many debilitating ways.

It was while at the kitchen table in his own home that he confessed his sins, recognizing idolatry for the first time. He renounced all spirits of divination related to his mother and the ouija board. I prayed, and Charlie was forthwith delivered from the demons of fear that he had picked up half a lifetime ago. The fearful attitudes that had undermined his entire being as a man vanished with those prayers.

Charlie's new joy and positive approach to life made him a different man for his wife and family to live with. His deliverance did wonders for his confidence as a self-employed tradesman.

People often express great surprise when learning that water-witching (water-divining) is a sin with grave significance. Because it is such a useful 'gift' to be found among rural people, I have often found Christians who have practised it. As the name shows, water-divining is a form of witchcraft or divination. Never mind that grandad and uncle Fred were deacons in the church and made a good supplement to their living by finding water sources under the ground. Those who have water-witches in their families are often afflicted with ills for which the only cure is by spiritual means, confession, repentance and deliverance.

A man came to see me who had until a few days before been employed as personal assistant to a leading medium in an Ontario city. He had helped her on occasions where the police had sought her psychic ability for assistance when investigating missing people or murder victims. The man told me how the medium worked, calling upon spirits for information that, more often than not, proved accurate. She amazed the officers, and took all the glory.

The assistant was a gifted water-witch and medium in his own right. Now he had met Jesus. He had come to seek deliverance from the many demons that had used and abused him for many years. I questioned his employer's successes for demons are king-size deceivers and liars. 'Ah! But they also have a network which is in touch with people's wickedness,' he said.

Human fascination with the unknown, the secret which belongs to God alone, is a continual source of satisfaction to the soul-destroying powers of darkness. Evil spirits wait, ever ready to pounce on the unwary, eager to insinuate themselves into minds of the almost innocent. I have often found that the key moment when a person's life started to go wrong was their involvement, perhaps naively, with psychic forces.

A young couple, Marjory and Rick, had recently taken three year-old Joey as a foster-child. Their pastor suggested they call me because the child was given to running around the house, screaming and shouting in a gruff voice. He would stop, and resoundingly bang his head on the floor. He did this repeatedly. The family physician could do nothing that helped.

The worried foster-parents told a sorry tale about this child. His mother was a prostitute who often suffered severe abuse from her clients. The Lord's pity flooded my heart. I sat the lad on my knee, and told him the Gospel story, and how Jesus had known all about him long before he was born, and loved him so much.

I laid my right hand on his head and commanded every evil spirit out, in the Name of Jesus. From that time on the boy behaved normally.

Before they took him home, I found out the couple had been Christians only a few years. I felt I should ask them if they had ever been involved in the occult.

'Yes,' Marjory answered. Then, 'I used to go every Wednesday evening to a woman's house where she held séances.'

I explained: 'Marjory, that practice was flat disobedience to the commandment of God, and very dangerous. You could still be suffering from the effects.'

No one had ever told her this before and she was quick to confess it as sin and renounce every spirit the séances had exposed her to. Upon my agreement with her and command that the demons should leave, Marjory sat bolt upright with a look of astonishment, and said graphically, 'I felt them go out of my gut!'

'Rick, did you ever go with your wife to a séance?' I asked.

'No, never. I thought the whole thing was nonsense! I used to take her, though, and sit in a room there, waiting for her.'

At my suggestion, Rick, an innocent bystander to his wife's

folly, gladly renounced the devil and any spirits he might have picked up at the medium's house. Upon deliverance prayer Rick exclaimed with amazement,

'Wow! I have had a ringing in my ears for years. The moment you told any spirits to leave, the ringing stopped!'

Our youngest daughter Alison was about fourteen when a friend invited her to an overnight slumber party. Before she went, I warned her to beware of a common occurrence at such parties:

'Alison, I hope you enjoy yourself. Watch out, however, if the girls start to talk about trying to do some magic, or have a séance.

'As soon as someone suggests that it would be fun to try to contact a dead grandma, or to have four girls put one finger under the corner of a sleeping bag to see if they can lift the girl off the floor, get out! Phone home and I will come and get you. Tell them what they are doing is wrong. Do not stay in the same room with your friends. Pray for the help of Jesus.'

Sure enough, about eleven o'clock Alison called home in tears. All she said was, 'Dad, please come and get me!' I picked her up, thinking that she might have felt ill. In the car she would not say anything until we were nearly home. Then it spilled out. The girls had started to talk about spirits and someone had suggested the levitation trick. When they started to scramble up from their sleeping-bags to try the 'magic,' Alison made her stand. The others laughed at her. However, my children were brought up in a home where God reigned supreme and where spiritual realities of good and evil were discussed over the table. Alison was in tears because her friends would not listen to her.

I telephoned the house and spoke to the host mother, for

she had thought Alison to be ill and was worried. When I explained what had happened, a querulous 'blank' came back over the line. The woman probably thought I was strange in the head. A pleasant person, she was worrying about a possible physical sickness in my child, yet she was totally impervious to the possibility of a spiritual sickness with eternal consequences for her own daughter, and the children of several other families.

Occult involvement can seriously affect all the members of a person's family and, I believe, many succeeding generations, as we shall see. I discovered this through prayer after many puzzling experiences with people who had kept clear of the occult yet had mysterious abilities in the realm of prognostication – 'seeing' the future.

Our second daughter, Helen, had a friend at university, Meg, who would suddenly look up and say, 'So-and-so will knock on the door.' A few seconds later, the rat-a-tat would echo down the hallway. Meg would tell fortunes for other women and sometimes be right in many details, to her 'client's' amazement. Sometimes she would be quite wrong. There was no dependability, but some people were fascinated and often came to her for advice.

Helen arranged a picnic when I could meet Meg. Casually, I said to her, 'I hear you have an interesting gift.' When she replied with a nod, 'Yes,' I asked her where she thought it had come from. 'It came from God,' she said, for she was a keen member of a Christian church.

To my question, 'Do you enjoy this gift?' Meg answered, 'No. I would rather I did not have it, but I suppose it must be for someone's good, mustn't it?'

Meg admitted that when clairvoyant thoughts came into her mind she did not know whether to speak about them or not. Sometimes they were ugly and menacing, or they could be happy and pleasing. Sometimes the thoughts were accurate about a future circumstance, and sometimes hopelessly incorrect. On balance, she would be very happy if God would take the gift away from her.

I asked if her mother had the same ability. 'Oh, yes! And my grandmother, too!' Meg explained that there was also a family ghost that had been in the farmhouse where she had been born. The strange thing was, the ghost had moved with the family when it relocated in town.

When I suggested that the fortune-telling spirit might not be from God, but from the devil, Meg perked up visibly. 'You mean, I *should* get rid of it? How can I do that? I have had it as long as I can remember.'

After some teaching, Meg gladly confessed her sin, and renounced the devil and her evil family inheritance. I prayed with the authority Christ has given to the church, and she was delivered. Meg jumped to her feet and ran off, dancing. 'I'm free!' she sang, 'I'm free!'

My experience with folk who have come under serious fortune-telling influence suggests that they can make significant decisions based on a clairvoyant's words. One woman, happily anticipating her marriage, changed her whole life when she broke her engagement on the strength of her astrological chart. Another person might become so full of fear that to make almost any decision becomes a frightening experience.

I used to ask myself, how it is that a clairvoyant can sometimes be strangely right and at other times definitely wrong? Then I met Phyllis, a hairdresser who loved her work, and whose customers loved her. She would often get pictures in her mind about a client and tell them what she saw. When she told a woman something that only the woman knew, her customer would be amazed, and ask for more insights. Gradually Phyllis built up a clientele which valued her almost as much for her fortune-telling as for her hairdressing.

Phyllis was a keen churchgoer, and after a serious mental breakdown received miraculous healing and baptism in the Holy Spirit. She came to me one day to tell me of her 'gift,' and her desire to be rid of it. Now she knew Christ in an intimate way and had found how totally trustworthy and consistent God is. The psychic 'gift' she had inherited from her mother was tawdry and darkly offensive to her spirit.

She related one frightening experience she had had while doing a customer's hair. Suddenly, she had 'seen' the woman's husband and son in a head-on collision at a precise bend in a certain country road. Knowing that this could be a 'false prophecy' she had held her tongue, not wanting to alarm her client. A few days later a head-on accident claimed the lives of the two men at the exact spot she had envisioned. Phyllis told me that, from the instant the precognition had come to her, she had thought about little else. She worried, dreading to hear the small town's radio news, 'in case.'

As I listened to her story, it came to me that Phyllis had actually been experiencing a fearful *faith* that her vision would come true. It seemed to me that, as Christ did great things because of a person's faith, the devil might also rely on human faith to accomplish some of his wicked deeds. Faith gives the spiritual realm 'purchase' in the physical world.

I came upon many people with occult gifts of divination, with this result: I became convinced that the devil can get many of his fortune-telling servants' prognostications right because he knows human nature so well. He often gets them wrong because what he foretells is blind, though intelligent guesswork. He does *not* really see into the future other than by clever surmise.

Satan does, however, clearly discern people whom he has affected and upon whom he has a hold. He continues to use or afflict them any way he can. These people may have 'asked' for him to get his hooks into them by their own evil curiosity, desire for occult power, or other sinful practice. Other folk may be in his clutches without ever having sought to break God's commandments, as we shall see.

~ 10 ~

The Sandwich-Board Phenomenon

A Picture of How the Devil Leaves His Mark

He was a serious-minded clergyman who combined a scholar's love of the Bible with a powerful faith that had led him into a full life, deep in the Spirit. Philip puzzled over the fact that, from time to time, men would proposition him as though he were a homosexual, which he was definitely not.

This was not the first time I had come across someone who felt threatened by evil-minded, sexually demanding people. I had heard of similar homosexual advances being made to men and women. The most frequent occurrences involved women who experienced sexual confrontation by men who seemed to consider their suggestions perfectly normal. They approached with assurance, even to the point of insistence, 'Surely?'

As I had often asked others, I asked if Philip could remember ever having been molested as a child, or in his teen years. At once there sprang to his memory a suppressed recollection of an older cousin, Keith, a boy who had pushed the young Philip into exposure and experimental sexual acts. He had experienced appalling guilt, his conscience stain-streaked. With innocence gone, Philip felt indescribably unclean. The young lad was frightened of his cousin and terrified to tell his parents.

Philip had never related his experience to anyone until my direct question. Tears sprang to his eyes. He hesitated, then described the event, and the shame and horror he had felt at the time. It still stuck in his soul like a poisoned barb. I could see Philip was living again the suffering of long ago.

'Philip,' I said, 'I believe there is a direct link between your childhood experience and the fact that to this day, you can find yourself in the appalling position of having to reject propositions or hints from homosexual men. In other words, what your cousin did all those years ago was enough to cause every problem you have had of this kind.

'The only way I can describe the effect of Keith's assault on you is to say that evil spirits were involved. They probably included Lust, Homosexuality, Incest and Sodomy. The spirits left unclean, spiritual "sticky finger-marks" upon you. From that time on you were a "marked man." It is as if you have been wearing a sandwich-board proclaiming to other evil spirits, *"Homosexual!"*

'Any practising homosexual carrying a homosexual spirit knows instinctively that you are "one of them." But, of course, you are not. But could there have been enough sin in you for the devil to implant curiosity, doubt and insecurity about your maleness?

'What happens is this: the homosexual spirit in the man recognizes the same kind of spirit sticking to you. That demon stirs up recognition in the homosexual's mind. It is a counterfeit of the Holy Spirit's gift of discernment. From then on, for the man, it is simply a case of his regular "pick-up-a-casual-lover" routine. He probably has no more idea that he has a demon in him than you, till now, have recognized that you had a demon accompanying you!'

Philip was amazed at the simple cunning of the evil spirit

world, and was ready instantly to put into words his sorrow for the sin to which he had (though unwillingly) allowed himself to be a party. With vehemence, he said, 'I renounce the devil and all his works, and every evil desire of the flesh!'

As I led him, Philip repeated, 'I renounce and bind every spirit associated with Keith my cousin, every unclean and homosexual spirit. I am a child of God, and I command you to go to the place prepared for you, now!' I uttered a similar command and smiled as I saw a look of relief spread across Philip's face.

'You know,' he said, 'I feel better already. I think my troubles are over.' And they were!

Much more frequently I have met females, from teenage girls through to mature women, who have found themselves 'marked' demonically. Once in 'sandwich-board' position, the spirits attract men to them like wasps to jam. Typically, their problem is that they experienced sexual abuse as children, often incestuously by a close relative, father, brother, uncle, cousin or even grandfather. Sometimes it has been a mother's 'boyfriend.'

Once having suffered from the lustful attack, whether molesting or something more serious, the girl has carried a spiritual stigma. This 'sandwich-board' is as plain to a demonized man or boy as if she had been branded on her forehead. Could human eyes have seen the mark she bore, it would have said 'Whore,' or 'Prostitute,' or simply 'Available.'

Some of these hurting women fall into practising sexual sin as a normal way of life, perhaps earning an income, if not their living, from it. By far the largest percentage, however, appear to become despised victims of male lust, violence and wickedness. Commonly, beginning in teenage, girls begin looking for love, and give their bodies to their boyfriends without hesitation. Disappointed by the fleeting nature of their 'relationship' they quickly turn to another male for what they yearn – true and constant love.

Their wonder is therefore very great when, after most of a lifetime as human sex-targets, they recognize the demonic nature of their wretchedness. Where it is necessary, individuals confess their own willing participation in sinful acts. If not already believers, they are always ready to believe that they have a true lover in the person of the Son of God. They learn for the first time that their Creator knows them intimately, and loves them with an everlasting love, shown by the Cross and Resurrection.

The first and necessary response to receiving the intimate and perfect love of Jesus is to ask him for forgiveness for their sins. Often people experience a struggle in matching Christ's offer of forgiveness with his insistence that they *give* forgiveness to those who offended them. This can mean releasing long pent-up bitterness and rage. Sometimes little girls have told their parents about the 'bad things' that 'Uncle Jack,' or 'Grandad' or a big brother did to them, only to have their heart's cry dismissed. The black burden of resentment against those parents is emotionally crippling. Those who should have come to their help with just anger and a deep, compassionate comfort failed. If this was love, what might God's love be like? Was he also as untrustworthy as Mummy and Daddy? The key to emotional healing lies in facing the reality of personal sin, and being honest about the failures of beloved others.

Peggy was a strong-willed Christian woman who had protected herself from subsequent immorality, though she had been molested by a relative. When she told her parents, 'they swept it away, and we all pretended it never happened.'

Peggy wrote, 'I had never been able to give my full trust to God, or to anyone, because trust had been repeatedly broken in my life as a child and adult. That day I was with you I forgave and began to trust. Since then, a new adventure has begun for me. Now I can love others even when I feel they violate me. I have a new passion to know God who is good, and can be trusted. He can give me joy and peace and hope in the midst of all life's struggles. God bless you. I am a happy child at last!'

A woman who has lived an immoral life can follow steps similar to those described for Philip, renouncing the devil and evil spirits associated with her behaviour, and commanding them to go. One of the greatest rewards of ministry is to see a female come out from under a huge weight of ruin, and then gain a wonderful self-esteem from the assurance of forgiveness and Christ's blessing.

Some women who have been given glorious liberty by Jesus go on to powerful ministry in his name. Ann, a prostitute who also sold drugs for her pimp, became a full-time counsellor working for a Christian psychotherapist. She led many people to personal faith in Christ, and then discipled them.

In the name of Jesus, the Liberator of all who come to him with faith, the demonic 'sandwich-board' becomes match-wood. That invisible 'mark' which called attention of other demons and their hosts to the suffering 'target' is eradicated. The invisible 'brand' is forever erased by the Name and Precious Blood of Christ who gives love, joy, peace and glorious hope, with holiness, to those who were so long bound in sin.

~ 11 ~

'Let the Little Children Come to Me' (Luke 18:16)

Jesus Saves Little Ones Tortured by Evil Spirits

Evil spirits can afflict children, as the story of Joey in chapter 9 shows. Appalling though the thought is, even the tiniest of infants can be affected by demons if they live in an atmosphere where people worship Satan, or where the commandments of God are dreadfully or continually broken. Because of a young child's immaturity it is not possible to take an infant through such an excellent process as Neil T. Anderson outlines in his *Steps to Freedom in Christ*.[1] It is quite out of the reach of a little person.

In dealing with children, Scriptural truth must be given to them at a level they can receive, which may be extremely limited. Then the counsellor exercises the ministry of exorcism for the child's benefit. Though Anderson says he thinks there is 'no such thing as an exorcist,'[2] I believe the power of Jesus' Name has to be exercised on behalf of a child who is too young to grasp his or her need for deliverance.

In the case of a baby, the intellectual ability to comprehend words of Gospel truth will be non-existent. However, I have seen God heal tiny ones of physical diseases and I always tell infants, even babies, the truths about Jesus and his love, the Cross and resurrection, before praying for them. My sense is that they receive a powerful anointing from his word.

I told the story of Jesus and his love to a two day-old baby girl. She was born with such severe haemophilia that the baby's unmarried mother had learned with horror that her child had a life expectancy of a maximum of three months. Within three days of my laying hands upon the child she was discharged from the hospital perfectly well, to the joy and astonishment of the hospital staff. Perhaps the truth about God's love is so powerful that it can be received spiritually, even though it is beyond mental grasp.

An older child who heard and believed the Gospel was Jane, not quite five years old. She had been adopted at eighteen months by Christian parents, whom she adored.[3] Her natural, unmarried mother and violent common-law father had forced the child to participate in sex-orgies. In that first year-and-a-half, Jane had also been subjected to ridicule and mockery. Then she was taken from the evil home.

A pretty child, Jane came to see me with her adoptive mother, their pastor and his wife. She was very full of herself, soon wanting to take control of my office, demanding paper, coloured crayons, pencils and pens. The pastor and Jane's mother came into my study while the pastor's wife took charge of the child and tried to keep her from too much mischief.

Jane's mother looked haggard and desperate after a long period of increasing hell at home with the girl. The child had been in continual care of psychiatrists and a mental health agency. Their diagnosis leaned towards 'multiple-personality' (some male and some female), and they had recommended that Jane be institutionalised for three months.

Seven days a week she was a spoiler, destroying her sister's toys and making the family's life intolerable. She spied and sneaked, and did mean tricks. She would follow her mother around the house and undo her housework so that it became useless to tidy up.

She spoke about 'the madness that is in me' which was 'a boy.' When someone tried to soften the word to 'badness' in her, she defiantly replied, 'No! It's madness!' She loved to be spanked and was glad if anything living suffered. She had tried to drown a cat and had deliberately attempted to drown her young cousin. ('Were you trying to teach Becky to swim, Jane?' 'No, I was trying to drown her!')

Jane's language was terrible, and when the 'madness' was upon her, her eyes went strange, and even her hair was 'different,' her mother said. She never showed remorse, often suffered from nightmares and, though she loved church, was always particularly wicked on Sundays.

Jane's harassed and worn out mother talked rapidly for an hour. I explained that her daughter was a classic example of someone who had been so exposed to evil that she had picked up demons. We could deal with them only in the authority of Jesus' Name and in the power of his Precious Blood.

The mother's eyes opened wide and the lines of exhaustion began to fade from her face. 'You are the first person to give me hope in all this time.' I told her the whole household would change as a result of what was going to happen. The chaotic Jane and the pastor's wife joined us in my study. I had the child sit between her mother and me so I could speak to her quietly and with her whole attention.

I spoke to her about sin, salvation, and the death and resurrection of Christ. I told of our need to be washed clean by his precious blood. Jane became very still. I told her that the devil had hurt her badly through certain people, and I named the natural parents and some others who had abused her.

'Jane, Jesus came into our world to save you and to destroy all the works of the devil. I want you to give your life to Jesus now, and I'm going to tell the devil and all that madness and badness, and sadness in you to go – and it will go. Right?' She nodded.

'I'm looking at you, Jane,' I said, looking into her earnest brown eyes, 'but I'm not talking to you. OK?' Then I prayed, 'Father, I thank you for your love for Jane and that she knows that Jesus came to give her life and freedom from all evil.'

I continued in a quiet voice, for demons can hear even a whisper, and if a command is impelled by faith they must respond. 'In the Name of the Lord Jesus Christ I bind every spirit that has been plaguing this little child whether you are outside her or within, and I command you to leave her and, harming no one, to go to the place prepared for you, now!'

The child sat very quietly and held her eyes tightly shut. I continued to her, 'Jane, think about Mary and Jake and Peter who hurt you so much and made you feel dirty inside, and about all the people who laughed and jeered at you. Jesus died on the cross for them, too, so they could be forgiven their sins. Can you forgive them, Jane?' She nodded. I said, 'God loves you so much, Jane. Do you want to love him too, and serve him as his little girl all your life?' She nodded again.

After I had prayed for her, I took a piece of paper and drew the outline of a cross with a little girl's face just under the crosspiece. 'There you are, Jane. That's you, right in the heart of Jesus. He will never leave you.' Jane smiled. On her way out of church she whispered, 'Mummy, the madness has gone now.'

Two days later Jane's mother called to say, 'Everything is wonderful. I cannot believe that only last week I wanted her to be placed elsewhere. The exciting thing is that my husband can sense that the evil has gone from this house. He says, "I have to rethink things!" Jane said to me, "I always knew it could be this way, that I could live with nice people." I cannot believe this is not a dream. I can give her crayons now and she will not immediately draw on the wall. I can leave her alone. She had her Daddy make a frame for her picture and put on it, "I belong to Jesus." '

Eight days later Jane's pastor reported, 'It has been a totally different week. Her father says he really must reexamine the claims of Christianity. The family is amazed.' Her mother wrote to me several months later, 'Jane is growing into a beautiful little girl. There are still problems as she learns to deal with the terrible abuse she suffered. The difference now is, she wants to be loving and caring for the sake of those close to her. Jane's words to me as I tucked her into bed this evening were, "I'm going to think of Jesus until I go to sleep." She thrives, knowing that Jesus loves her.' In the years which followed, Jane continued in her new life, a person changed by the liberating power of Jesus, her Saviour.

Paul was nine years old and could not speak, and was unable to dress himself. He shuffled into my study with his adoptive parents. His face was expressionless and foolish looking. His hands were practically useless and he had to be spoon-fed. While his parents outlined Paul's tragic infancy, I watched him playing on the floor with some little cars and trucks, pushing them around with the backs of his hands.

Obviously, Paul had suffered immense abuse from his natural parents, and it was just as clear that his adoptive mother and father loved him greatly. They were frustrated that nothing had helped their son grow out of babyhood though their medical advisors said there was nothing wrong with his brain.

I told Paul the timeless story of God's love in Christ, as he had been told often before, at home. I took him on my knee and bound the demons afflicting him and commanded them from his life. Then I prayed, blessing him and laying hands on his head. He smiled.

When it was time to go, Paul's father surprised himself, and his wife and me, by saying to his son, 'Paul put on your shoes.' Astounded, we watched as the little boy put on his shoes. Then, while we looked on in utter amazement, he carefully tied his shoe laces! The last I saw of Paul was his jaunty walk as he swaggered down the steps from my house, his hands in his pockets, whistling tunefully. His parents simply wept.

The spirits of Rejection and Rebellion are like a coin's head and tail. They are two sides of Satanic attack against many children, particularly those who feel rejected by their father and mother.

Ben was six when his mother called urgently. 'I know you have said you will not see anyone else from the church we belong to until you have met the pastor. But he is putting it off, and we have a son with terrible problems, and we have heard you could probably help. He has wet the bed every night of his life. He has no friends. His language is terrible, and he shouts and screams. Last week, for the third time, he ran away. He is intelligent but he cannot read or write. He knows the alphabet, but cannot read letters or numbers, yet he can do sums in his head. His teachers say he is uneducable. Ben causes endless trouble at school, and the authorities say he has to be put into an institution where he will probably spend the rest of his life.'

My first question was, 'Is he adopted?' He was not, so then I asked, 'Did you want him?'

'Oh, yes!' his distressed mother replied, to which I asked, 'Did you ever consider aborting him?'

'Well, as a matter of fact, yes. We already had two daughters and thought we could not afford another child, so the doctor had agreed to arrange an abortion, but we changed our minds.'

'It sounds as if he *could* be under demonic influence,' I said. I was thinking of spirits like Rejection and Rebellion which can easily enter the scene where abortion, or the disposal of living children, is planned. 'I will see your child, providing both you and your husband bring him, and you have the blessing of your pastor. And by the way, is Ben a believer?'

His mother answered, 'Oh, yes. He gave his life to Jesus when he was quite small, and he says his prayers every night before bed. He loves to go to church.'

A smartly dressed couple, Myra and Al, appeared on my doorstep a few days later with their lad. Ben was one of those frantically active and diverted children who could not sit still. As I tried to get his attention I remember feeling, with a wave of unreasonable aggressiveness, 'If *I* were six years old, I would punch this kid on the nose!' Now that was a strange thing! I have never been much of a nose puncher! I knew that this was an evil impulse generated by evil associated with the child.

It took several minutes to get him to pay heed to me. I established that he did believe in Jesus, and had a good understanding about sin, forgiveness, the Cross and resurrection. Furthermore, coming from a Pentecostal home, he had a good sense of the reality of the Holy Spirit. I was impressed. Finally, I said:

'Ben, who loves you?'

'Jesus!' he replied enthusiastically.

'Who else loves you?'

'Mum and Dad!' Ben said with a smile and equal enthusiasm.

'Yes, that's right, Ben. However, there is someone else who does not love you. Indeed, he hates all little children, and that is Satan.' Ben looked solemn; he had quietened down and was paying full attention now. I began to explain:

'Ben, your Mummy and Daddy love each other. Before you were born, and when they were very close together' (I held my hands up, palms together), 'a seed from your Daddy and one from your Mummy joined together, and there was the beginning of Ben, deep inside your Mummy. God gave that seed life, the spirit of Ben came from God and there you were, very, very small. You were meant to grow until you could be born into the world. Now when you were about this big' (I showed him my forefinger and thumb about an inch apart), 'your Mum found out she was going to have a baby.

'She and your Dad were very surprised and said, "But we don't want another baby, we have already got two little girls!" So they went to the doctor. He agreed to take that tiny little person (you) out of your Mummy so that the baby would not be born. But then Mummy and Daddy prayed, and after a few days, they changed their minds. "Why!" they said. "We might have a little boy, and call him 'Ben.' We will have this baby after all!"'

'Well, Ben,' I continued, 'When the devil learned at the beginning that they were going to have the doctor destroy that little baby, he was very glad. He knew that God, by his Spirit, had given you life and, because he hates all the good things God does, wanted your spirit to feel hated. So he sent a couple of demons to tell you bad things. They came along and said things like this to that tiny baby, "You are no good! No one wants you! They hate you!" and these evil spirits have been with you ever since.'

His parents and I gasped when Ben looked straight at me, and said, 'I know that. That's why I ran away last week!'

I called him across to me, with his parents' consent, and he willingly came and sat on my knee. 'Ben,' I said, 'we are going to tell those lying, evil spirits to leave you once and for all. OK?' 'Yes!' he replied.

'I am going to pray. Father, thank you that before Ben's mother and father came together, you had already planned to send his living spirit to give life to their seed. You knew he was going to be one of *your* children. You have always loved him, and will love him for ever. Now Father, in the Name of Jesus your Son we bind the evil spirits that have harmed your child Ben. I am now speaking to the spirits. I bind every spirit of Fear, Rejection and Rebellion, every unclean spirit and spirit of Self-hatred, Ignorance, Blindness and Evil Speaking, and command you to leave this boy, now!'

I gently laid my right hand on the boy's head, continuing, 'And we ask you, Lord Jesus Christ, who shed your precious blood for Ben, to bless this little boy and fill him with your Spirit. Bless him so that he will go on and grow up in your kingdom and follow you all the days of his life; make him a good son to his parents and good brother to his sisters; open his eyes so that he may read, and sharpen his understanding so that he may learn all that he needs to do well at school; and give him true friends, for your love's sake. Amen.'

I reached for the pad upon which I make notes. I wrote 'C-A-T.' 'What does that say, Ben?' I asked. 'Cat!' he replied. I put down some numbers for a simple addition sum and, in a twinkling, he had the answer.

These events took place on a Monday. Four days later, on Friday, I answered the telephone to hear the excited voice of Myra, Ben's mother. 'I hardly know where to begin! Ben has not wet the bed all week, and he has not used any bad language at all! Thursday he brought home a boy from school, his first friend ever. The Principal at school told me this tonight, "It looks as if our methods are at last working. I do not think Ben will have to be institutionalised, after all." I tell you, Mr Mitchell, our lives have changed round completely. We are *so happy!*'

Separation from one's parents is a very traumatic event. Children who spend time in foster homes, or who are eventually adopted, suffer emotional stress as all authorities recognize. What people do not understand is the devil's delight with every family that suffers breakup and chaos. Invisibly and effectively he is active behind many of these catastrophes in ways we are learning to discern.

Dealing with adopted children of all ages, from the very young to the elderly, I have come to appreciate that the demonic effects can last a lifetime. While Rejection and Rebellion are the biggest elements in the spiritual attack, Anger, Self-pity, Rage and Fear are representatives of other typical, lasting problems. I have often met parents who have an adopted child whom they have treated in every way like other children in the family, but who has given them terrible trouble. Sometimes the child has not even known it was adopted.

The best antidote to troubles of this nature is to meet them early. Whenever I know of adoptions I keenly suggest that prayers should be offered as soon as the baby or child is brought home. The prayers are simple. The parents state their trust and faith in God and their thanksgiving for the gift of the child. Together with them, I bind every evil spirit that has come upon the child from the moment of conception.

Next, I command those spirits to depart, now, to the place prepared for them. All inherited evil spirits are told they must release their hold on the child. We plead the Blood of Christ between this child and all his or her ancestors. Then we bless the child and commit it first into the hands of the Almighty forever, and then to the new parents for life. Whenever this has been done, the adopted children have grown up exactly like other children and have been no problem to anyone, including themselves.

My conclusion is this: Children can be affected by demonic forces whenever the God-designed relationship of marriage is seriously fractured. This can take place, for example, when a child becomes separated from its parent(s) because they have been vehemently at odds with each other. It can happen where a child has been conceived out of wedlock, denied by its father, and removed from its mother. Rejection comes upon such a child with feelings of worthlessness. A mother strongly rejects her child, sometimes from the minute she first realises she is pregnant ('Oh God! I don't want a baby!'). That attitude so offends the design of nature that it may allow supernatural evil to penetrate.

A child who has been rejected in the womb stands a good chance of entering the world as a strong-willed child who is crying for recognition as a person. 'I am *not* "worthless," "unwanted," "despised," or "rejected."' He fights violently against feelings that came to him by the circumstances that surrounded him before birth. Such a child is crying out from the heart, 'I *AM* SOMEONE! YOU CANNOT IGNORE ME! I *WILL* HAVE YOUR ATTENTION! I *WILL* GET MY

WAY! I'LL SHOW YOU I *AM* SOMEONE!' And that is, of course, the truth.

The problem is, the child is a natural-born sinner like everyone else coming into the world, and he or she enters with a spiritual 'chip on his shoulder.' The results can be heartbreaking for all who have to deal with him, and will work to turn the growing child into a rebel and troublemaker.

This destructive and self-damaging tendency is often concealed through outward compliance until the boy or girl reaches teenage years. The child's loving parents cry, 'We don't know what has got into him. He was always such a good boy, never gave us any trouble. All our children were treated the same way. He·was no exception. They always got on well. Now look at him! He believes in Jesus but he is turning away from God. What *can* we do?'

The answer is, deal with him as someone who, for no fault of his own, became demonically affected probably before he was even born. Speak to him as I spoke to little Ben (above), making appropriate changes according to the child's age and experience of life. I make this comment because I have dealt with adopted children, or those who have gone through severe childhood trauma of all ages. By the time I met them, some were already themselves grandparents.

A child in the womb may be able to receive demonic input from trauma other than emotional rejection. An elderly couple from a very conservative church background approached me with a story of great sadness. Hugh and Elizabeth had been Christians since childhood. Their five children had all been brought up in the faith. The first three children and the fifth child, now all married with their own families, had contented lives. The problem was child number four.

This woman, Penelope, now thirty-five, had entered the world screaming. Ever since, she had been a bad tempered and difficult person, totally at variance with her parents and siblings. She had married while still very young. When she was thirty, and without children, her husband was involved in a car accident. He was permanently crippled and his personality changed from injuries received to his head. From the beginning of his troubles his wife had shown that she wanted nothing to do with him now. Her parents were shocked at her callousness when she quickly divorced the suffering man.

It did not take the outwardly attractive Penelope long to find another mate. Having caught him, she reverted to character and made the man's life a horror with her rages and vicious tongue. It was at this stage that her parents came to see me.

I listened with great interest. I asked the usual question, 'Did you really *want* this child?' to which they answered in unison, 'Yes!' For the next two hours I probed into the family history, especially during the nine months of Elizabeth's pregnancy. No matter how we looked at the facts, it seemed the mother had carried the baby with the same degree of care, eager anticipation and love that typified all the other children's gestation. Hugh and Elizabeth and I prayed and kept silent, grasping for anything that might explain why one child out of five should be such a misfit.

Elizabeth looked up and quietly said, 'You know you asked if I had been involved in any accident while I was carrying her, and I said no. Well, I have just remembered something that happened when I was about seven months pregnant, though you could hardly call it an accident. We had a ladder into the basement of the house we lived in those days. Once

I was going down and missed my footing. I slipped down about three steps. I landed on my feet, but the fall really shook me up. I worried I might have hurt the baby, but all was well. I had forgotten all about the incident until we were praying just now. I wonder if that fall means anything?'

I was excited by this revelation which seemed to be a gentle reminder from God. I said, 'This is all we have to go on. I am going to assume that as you fell a spirit nearby leaped into action and began to harass the unborn child, saying, for example: "There you are you see, she hates you. She's trying to kill you!" If you agree, we will deal with the spirits that might typically be in a situation like that, Fear, Hatred, Rejection, Rebellion, Anger, and so on.'

Until this evening, Hugh and Elizabeth had thought that demons were simply an olden-days' way of describing mental and physical disorders. They had no idea that there might actually be real evil spirits active in the twentieth century. This was not anything their church had taught about.

Because there was no way they could get Penelope to meet me, we decided we would remember how Christ dealt with the Syrophoenician woman's demonized daughter (Mark 7:24-30), and pray from a distance. Penelope lived forty miles from my home. We prayed with as much faith as we could, that this child of God should be set free. We bound the spirits and commanded them to leave Penelope. Her parents, who said a loud 'Amen' to the prayers, found this kind of ministry very perplexing and left, I think, shaking their heads. And who could blame them?

The clincher came by way of a letter some six months later. Hugh wrote: 'It is amazing. From the day we prayed with you for Penny she began to change. Now, all this time later, she is more like the daughter we always knew she could be.

It is wonderful, now, to see her happier than she has ever been. We are all rejoicing, especially her husband. Recently we told Penny how we prayed that night. She was astonished, and she put her life anew into the hands of God.'

God looks at all people everywhere, however young or old, and loves them as their Father, wanting them to experience the fullness of life as children of God. Jesus is present wherever his name is invoked, ready to bless and act with grace and power. How precious his eternal word is:

'Let the little children come to me, and do not hinder them, for the kingdom of God belongs to such as these (Mark 10:14). . . . *If I drive out demons by the finger of God, then the kingdom of God has come to you'* (Luke 11:20).

Notes
1. Anderson, Neil T., *The Bondage Breaker* (Eugene, OR: Harvest House, 1990), 185.
2. ibid., 205.
3. The story of Jane first appeared in the 2 March 1988 issue of *Alliance Life*, under the title, 'Deliver Us from Evil!'

~ 12 ~

Ghosts – and Things Like That

They Really Do Exist

Why is it that children love to scare themselves with stories about ghosts? Every year at Hallowe'en so many dress up in scary clothes and faces. Perhaps children know there is a great deal in the world to be afraid of, so they compensate for the horrid reality by contriving horror that they can control? They know their ghosts and goblins are only 'pretend' and therefore safe.

However, fascination for ghost stories appears to be universal, a basic element in the human condition. In every culture, stories about the spirits of the dead abound. Many have received considerable credence, and often from people who can by no means be called simple-minded or uneducated. Back in England I was visiting the engineer-inventor priest who was at the time vicar of a parish in Gloucestershire. I learned from him and his sensible wife that the vicarage had a distinguished guest, the ghost of an eighteenth century bishop of Worcester who had been visiting when he died there.

Now the vicarage was a huge rambling place with its basic building dating from the thirteenth century. Additions had been made so that it had so many wings and rooms that it could have been turned into a country hotel. The only way the vicar could afford to live in it was because he had a private income from his inventions. I stayed overnight, enjoying wonderful hospitality. Next morning at breakfast I laughingly said, 'Well, I didn't see the bishop last night!' The straight and offhand reply of the minister came through a mouthful of toast and marmalade: 'Of course not. You were in the nineteenth century wing. Your room wasn't built till a hundred years after he died.'

A few miles south of Georgian Bay, Ontario lies an old family-farm. Peter and Mary had lived in a large city for many years where he had been a high school principal. When they retired, they found they could purchase the farm, which had belonged to his family for several generations.

The couple undertook a number of renovations which included the replacement of the old staircase with a fine new one of highly polished oak. After several months of uninterrupted and happy living in their new home, the couple awoke in the middle of the night to the sound of hobnailed boots clumping up the staircase. Peter, fearful and yet angry, leapt out of bed, turning on the light. On the landing, there with the lights blazing he saw ... nothing.

The phenomenon continued every night for several days until Peter called, to tell me the story. That afternoon I inspected the stairs. I could not imagine it possible for anyone in genuine hobnailed boots to climb them without spoiling the new and glistening surface. Mary was quite indignant. 'I heard them too, you know! We didn't imagine them!'

The three of us sat down and prayed, asking the Lord to show us what the problem was. I stood up and can only say that I felt impelled to go to the back door of the farmhouse. There, looking out over the yard I had a prickly sense of evil which I have learned to recognize as the presence of spirits.

While this sounds frightening, I can only assure readers that, because it is an awareness brought to one by the Holy Spirit who is all-powerful, the sensation is far from alarming. It includes a sense of outrage that the devil would dare to offend God's children; it contains an impression of the holiness of the Righteous One who delivers us from evil. In this instance I firmly and powerfully announced to whatever dark spirits were troubling the house and its owners that they had no right to do so. 'I bind you in the Name of Jesus Christ, the Lord of heaven and earth, and I command you never to come here again. Go to the place prepared for you. Amen!' From then onwards Peter and Mary enjoyed peace in their delightful home.

Another noisy, foot-clumping spirit troubled a young couple who lived in the southern Ontario town of Tillsonburg. Ann and Warren had been married a few years when I talked to Ann at the drive-in restaurant where she worked. I could see she was unhappy and I asked her about it. 'Oh, this is the worst day of my life! When I finish my shift in a few minutes, I am going home to move out. We cannot live together any longer! Our baby is in a hospital and is not responding to treatment, and Warren is terrible about *everything*! We cannot stand each other!'

I asked Ann if I could give her a ride home. On the way I listened to her and found myself invited into the living room which opened directly from the central front door. Just beyond was the kitchen where I could see random piles of unwashed dishes and pans, and opened cans of food. The place was very dirty and untidy. Scattered around the living room were sex magazines, some lying open.

I talked to Ann about the grace of Jesus who came into the world to save her, Warren, and her baby for the fullness of life. She listened and slowly her tears dried up. She dabbed at her bottom eyelids in the way women do. I could see that she was ready to ask forgiveness of God and to put her life into his hands.

At that very moment the front door burst open and in came her husband in dirty jeans and tee-shirt, all fitness and bulging muscles. There I was, sitting beside his wife on the sofa! I leapt to my feet! I said, very quickly, 'Hi! You must be Warren. I am a minister and we were just talking about how Jesus wants to clean up the awful mess you are in, and heal your daughter too. What do you think about that?'

To my astonishment, the man replied, 'If that is true, it is the most wonderful thing I have ever heard!' Within the next few minutes I had fully explained the Gospel again. The couple knelt side by side and asked forgiveness of all their sins. They told God they wanted him to rule their lives. 'Oh Lord, help us!' Then they faced one another, still on their knees and asked for, and gave, forgiveness to each other. They wept and clung together. I prayed for them both, laying hands on them and asking God to fill them with his Holy Spirit, and asked God to heal their baby lying in the hospital. They gave a loud 'Amen.'

Two days later I visited the home and found a colossal change had taken place. The rooms were spotless. Ann and Warren were arm-in-arm, smiling joyfully. Their baby was peacefully sleeping on a blanket, surrounded by toys. She had wonderfully healed at the hour her parents and I had prayed for her to their heavenly Father. And they had this news for me:

'Neither of us had ever told the other about this, but we both had heard strange things in this house. Every day the front door used to sound as if it was opening and then slamming shut. Footsteps would come stomping through the living room, up the hall and into the bathroom with a bang. It was always the same: no one was there and the doors did not move. We both thought that if we said anything the other would think we were crazy! The thing is, though, ever since you were here and we invited Jesus to be Lord of our lives, the whole performance has stopped dead.'

As we thanked God for this, along with all the other blessings, I could not help thinking that an evil spirit had been at work through the whole affair. It had not only made noise, it had done evil toward the child by sickness, the husband by unclean thoughts, the wife by despair, and overall had brought confusion and destruction to their home and marriage. This is the way demons work, and this one had been sent flying by the faith and repentance of two souls bent on following the Truth, Jesus Christ the Lord of heaven and earth.

The western folklore is that ghosts, such as that of the old Bishop of Worcester who was mentioned earlier, are the spirits of dead humans. These are restless spirits that remain somehow anchored to earth until released from it by prayers, or some other method, so that they can then depart and go to their rest. In other parts of the globe 'wandering spirits' may be identified as demons or gods. They conjure up fear and anxiety, and are often tricky, mischievous or spiteful. Placating the spirits plays a significant part in many forms of religion.

The notion in western culture is that spectres, and subtle presences which communicate personality, are indeed the spirits of deceased people. I have difficulty with this tradition on the basis that '... *man is destined to die once, and after that to face judgment*' (Heb. 9.27). I can find nothing in the

Scriptures that shows anything other than the fact that the spirits and souls of the righteous and the unrighteous are in the hand of God. A person dies, and their spirit and soul return to their maker.

There is historic and contemporary evidence that wickedness occurring in or characterizing a person's life, can somehow continue after his death. Effects are felt by a relative, or a person who resides in the deceased's dwelling. There continues to be an 'atmosphere' or sensation of evil which induces similar behaviour, or at least a fear of that dead person. I have learned to treat such 'ghostly' manifestations as if they are demonic rather than human. Let me explain:

There is no doubt in my mind that evil spirits are often at work tempting, goading and energizing fear or evil in people. Demons seek humans as their hosts, just as canine fleas seek dogs to be their hosts. When a dog dies, it leaves its fleas alive and in need of a new host. When a person dies who has been affected by demons he or she has 'picked up,' those evil spirits still have their work to do. They hang around their host's 'old haunts' and seek another host. Sometimes they will be satisfied with simply remaining in the location to mystify, scare and intrigue humans, thus pulling their attention away from the One Spirit who is worthy of attention, Almighty God and his Son Jesus Christ. By their appearances from time to time, or other manifestations, such as moving objects around, or producing aromas or sounds, they appeal to the human need by causing counterfeit spiritual 'refreshment' or interest. In other words, ghosts are the devil's agents to draw attention to him and away from Jesus.

I have satisfied myself that this is true by dealing with ghostly phenomena as demonic and not as the evidence of the continuing presence of tragic human figures. Ghosts are more likely to be spirits that were familiar with the deceased, 'familiar' spirits. They were actively involved in the person's life either to abuse him or her, or to use the person in the doing of evil of some kind. Someone has said that 'familiar' spirits are so called because, without discernment, they feel familiar and right. In each instance the aim would be to spoil, corrupt and besmirch the person's character and thus hinder the loving work of Christ in the 'host' and in anyone else that person might affect for ill, one way or another.

Rather than offering prayers for the deceased person's rest (he has already gone on to his Creator), I would pray for the removal of the evil spirit that accompanied the person in life. I would declare it bound in heaven and on earth in the name of Jesus Christ the Lord of heaven and earth, and would command it to go immediately to the place prepared for it. Another story will illuminate what I mean:

A few years ago my wife and I were visiting relatives in England when I found myself spending a very interesting evening with their minister. As a result, he arranged for me to accompany him when he visited a couple who had come into a large sum of money and had built themselves a grand new home in the village. Phillip and Doris were pleasant people, enjoying a new time in their lives. No, they did not consider themselves to be real Christians, they only went to church occasionally, and no, they were not in the habit of praying. But they did have a problem in this fine new house – the ghost of Doris' mother!

When the couple moved in, they brought with them old Mrs Smith. She had lived with them a year before dying peacefully in the night. Now, she was a good woman without any evil ways, 'though she did say that she saw things other people did not see, people's fortunes, and things like that.' Mrs Smith was very fond of jasmine scented perfume. Ever since she had died, her daughter and son-in-law had been aware of her presence coming into a room because of the aroma of jasmine which had always typically announced her presence in life. I expressed my views that the scent might indicate an evil spirit which had troubled Mrs. Smith during her life, quite possibly a spirit of divination (fortune-telling).

I talked to Phillip and Doris about God's love for them personally and before too long they knelt on the luxurious carpet in their living room and gave their lives to the service of Christ, asking for forgiveness of all their sins through the Cross and Passion of Jesus. From their kneeling position they suddenly looked at each other with alarm. With one voice they said, *'She's here!'*

Gently (there is no need to shout and get excited about such a normal part of the Christian ministry as delivering people, or places, from demonic bondage), I said: 'Spirits associated with Doris' mother, Mrs Smith, you have heard the confession of these two people. They are children of the Most High and you have no right to afflict them any more. You are bound, and I command you to leave them and this place, and go to the place prepared for you, *now!* Amen.' In that instant the aroma of jasmine left the room. Doris' and Phillip's eyes opened wide with amazement; then their relief spread across their faces in beams of joy.

We all got to our feet, rejoicing, for this small incident had taken place while we were still kneeling. The ghost of Mrs Smith had been an evil spirit all the time, not the disembodied human soul of Doris' mother. It had put on its 'appearance' at the very second the couple had finished committing their lives to Christ, no doubt to distract them and confuse the plain issue of who was to have spiritual authority in their lives, Christ or the demon. Now the deceiving spirit had gone forever!

A young couple, not long married, were living in the upstairs apartment of an older house in a small village in Oxford County, Ontario. At a Bible study and prayer meeting for young adults, the husband related how he and his bride constantly experienced a 'presence' in their first home. It seemed to follow them around. It had never appeared to them, or made any noises, or done any other spooky stuff. Enough that it was there!

That evening, when we came to the time for prayers, we addressed the spiritual realm in the mighty name of Jesus, bound the spirit at the couple's address, commanded it to stop harassing them, and go to the place assigned for it. When the young husband got home, his wife greeted him with, 'Guess what! The thing has gone!' 'Guess what!' he replied. 'It went about nine-thirty, didn't it?' There was great rejoicing at the grace of the Lord Jesus Christ that night. He watches over us. His angels are his ready ministers to help God's people. All he is waiting for is for his people to take his word seriously . . .

In the same part of southwestern Ontario lived a United Church pastor and his wife and family. My wife and I had grown very close to them as we were alongside them through some difficult times. Angus had received the baptism of the Holy Spirit one day when I was praying for him and since then, he had found his ministry coming to glorious life. One night, while he was leading a Bible study in his manse, a loud knocking came on his door. There were three people: an old bent, white-haired man and two teenagers, all looking very troubled.

'Can you come out right now to a farm near here? There's a man ill in bed and a spirit has come and talked to him from the foot of his bed. It said, "Tonight, you are going to die!" He is terrified. He sent us out to get a minister. We did not know where to go, then we thought of you.'

Angus phoned me to tell me what had happened. 'David, this sort of thing is all beyond me. Is there any chance you can come out to help?' I sped as quickly as I could through the darkening evening.

Bundling the old man and young people into my car with Angus in the front to guide me through the early spring countryside, we approached the run-down farm buildings. I had an intense feeling that we were going into a spiritually dark area. Inside, no paint showed on the long-neglected walls, the rough floor was dirty and a pot-bellied stove glowed in the middle of the room. It appeared that a crowd of young people had taken over a derelict place and had moved in to live there.

With scared faces crowding round the frame of the door into the afflicted man's ground-floor bedroom, Angus and I began to question him. This was the leader of the little commune. Yes, he was a believer and no, he had never been involved in the occult. He had been feeling sick but thought it was just 'flu, or something like that. He had been getting worse all day when this spirit appeared and nearly scared the life out of him. We made sure that he was up to date with his confession and had nothing outstanding between him and God. He was right with everyone else, too, as far as he knew.

I went back into the room and spoke to all the people. 'If any of you are committed Christians, if you truly believe in the Lord Jesus Christ and have given your life to him, you can stay here. If not, I want you out of here and right off the property. Your friend is in a bad way and we have to help him immediately.' They scooted out of there like a bunch of frightened rabbits.

Angus and I stood on the front porch of the old house. We could make out white faces over the gate into the farmyard. I began to speak in a firm and audible voice so that it would echo round what I took to be a fairly small property. 'In the name of the Lord Jesus Christ we address every evil spirit on this property. You have no right here: it is under the leadership of a Christian man. We command you to leave this place and stop afflicting a servant of God!'

We went back inside and, after we had made certain that we had dealt with any demons that might still possibly be hanging around the room or the patient, prayed for the ill man, anointing him in the name of the Lord. He immediately felt better and began to struggle weakly out of bed. We called the group back inside into the large warm room.

I looked across at the old, bent, white-haired man who had come with the two teenagers to Angus for help, and felt God speaking clearly to me. First of all I addressed the assembled band of dishevelled young people. I told them exactly what had happened, that the authority of the Saviour of the world had rid the place of troubling spirits. I gave them the Gospel story briefly, and told them that they should all take this chance of settling in their own minds the need to repent and receive Christ as Saviour and Lord. Then I spoke to the old man. I had rarely spoken with such forceful words in my whole life. '*As for you, my friend, you must make up your mind very soon. You do not have much longer!*' This was the word that the Lord had given to me. I was never so certain of anything, yet I found myself wondering at the boldness with which I spoke.

Driving home much later that night, I was considering the craftiness and power of the enemy which had brought one man to be sure that he was at the brink of death, and which had also impressed me with the sense of permeating evil in the house and property. Then, suddenly, I saw a demon curled up on the floor of the passenger side of my car. It appeared as a writhing, Chinese-style dragon, blue-green and luminous and about two feet long. In the same instant I recognized my sin and breathed a prayer of repentance for succumbing to fascination with evil. The thing vanished in a split second, and I went on my way rejoicing and singing praises to our wonderful God. Hallelujah! How great he is!

About two weeks later I was coming out of my office when an elderly and erect, military-like man came smartly across the street to me. He said, 'I took your words seriously! Last week I went to a meeting in Aylmer where I gave my life to the Lord, and I was healed! Hallelujah!' People in the street looked up, wondering what the noise was about. If they could have seen the bent and perplexed old man as I had seen him that night not long ago, and now recognized this as the same person, saved and delivered from a crippling spirit of infirmity, *they* would have shouted too!

~ 13 ~

These Premises May Be Bugged
Evil Spirits at Work in Church Buildings and Private Homes

hrist's and our adversary, the devil, is crafty. He is also predictable. The problem is, until we have learned how he operates, we cannot anticipate him or even recognize his activity when he is at work. God may, however, give warning by divine revelation, though this is unusual. He has given us the Bible and the Church, and those, for the wise, are generally sufficient.

The Lord must surely expect us to use every gift of the Spirit to develop spiritual sensitivity. Then we can be prepared to do combat with the foe both defensively and offensively. Part of our learning process should include how he operates against churches, their buildings and through them against their Christian communities. Then we will be able to counteract his efforts and get the glory for Jesus.

Satan sends his spiritual emissaries into churches. Sometimes these are in human persons according to Mylander[1] and others. Once I was helping a pastor who was having tremendous difficulties with many individuals and groups in his large and highly respected church. It had fallen on hard times, and no one could understand why.

As he and I, and several leaders, prayed our way through the maze of the facilities I was alert for the giveaway sensation that confirms to me the presence of evil spirits. In this room and that I could say, 'this room is OK,' or 'there are problems here.' Every time we sensed demonic influence the pastor and his wife named the specific individuals who were engaged in a ministry in that particular work area and who had become extremely difficult in recent years. Finally, in the boardroom it was as if we had walked into a large angry nest of spirits. It was like 'hearing' hell's bells.

Later, I felt I ought to spend time in the sanctuary where I was drawn into the balcony, to a specific seat. There I found myself sensing the whole auditorium filled with people for an evangelistic rally. It was on such a night, the date of which came into my mind, several years earlier that an unknown man, with a specific name which also came clearly to my mind, had come with the intention of drawing demons into the sanctuary to begin work on the destruction of the church. Could the deep troubles that were facing the pastor and threatening to destroy his ministry and the fine name of the church have stemmed from the visit of such a man on that particular night? Is such a thing possible?

I believe such a thing could happen. Therefore I make it a practice to take necessary steps to evict any undesirable spirits from any church I have to do with, and to defend against their entry. But why do I think evil spirits attempt to gain access into churches? Not a difficult question! Satan wants to undermine the work of the Spirit in the congregation's life. He aims to sow trouble of many sorts and so disable as many personal relationships as he can, and to slow down the pace of productive discipleship.

Remember – the devil is the arch-deceiver, called by Jesus *'the father of lies,'* a spoiler and wrecker with aeons of accumulated finesse. Satan is adept at his skills of robbing, murdering and destroying (John 10:10). For example, *if he can*, he will 'steal' the word of God so that people do not *receive* the truth from a sermon even though they may *hear* the words that the preacher says; he will sow discord in any Christian group and so 'murder' relationships; he will keep the church poor and constantly rob it of funds; he will destroy the peace that passes all understanding . . . and so on . . . *if he can.*

The snag is, problems such as these seem so much part of 'normal' church life that they are often accepted as nothing extraordinary. We expect them! To that compliant attitude I say, 'NONSENSE!' Such unhappiness, the spoiling of true joy in a congregation, is evidence that the enemy of our souls is at work. The pity is, all too often he stays unidentified.

Even if believers sense that the devil is at work, they don't know what to do about it. They have been conditioned to 'put their head down' and struggle on. They have not been taught how to 'grasp the nettle,' face the spiritual reality and (to mix my metaphors) beat it down under their feet. But when the church does recognize the spiritual nature of its distress, victory can be very near.[2] All it needs is for the grace and power of God to be appropriated, as this story shows:

The new pastor had spent some years as an evangelist. He knew how to preach and move people to respond. His first sermon to a full congregation seemed to 'bounce back' into his face. As the people left church they smiled politely and shook his hand and said trifling things about the weather and it was nice to see him.

During the week he prayed, mystified at their blankness. He carefully prepared for his next sermon. Again, he met a wall of resistance. They did not seem to have heard a word he said. So he prayed to God and asked, *'What is the matter with them, or is it with me?'* It seemed to him that the Lord replied, *'The problem is not with you, or the people. It is the church. It is full of religious spirits.'* The pastor said, 'During the following week I prayed all through the church, pleading the Blood of Christ over every corner and throughout the sanctuary, commanding every evil spirit out of the place in the Name of Jesus. I went up and down the rows of pews claiming the Precious Blood over each seat. And I blessed everywhere after it had been cleansed. Next Sunday, revival broke out!'

I was speaking to this pastor's successor some ten years later. He told me the congregation was one of his denomination's outstanding churches in the province.

On one occasion a young minister sought an appointment for me to suggest how he might assist an ex-Satanist to clean up her life. He brought a large woman into my study and explained how she had been at his church now for several weeks. Now she wanted to become a Christian.

As I considered the woman, I became convinced that she was a fraud. I said, 'I think you are lying. The reason you started at the church was that you were told to find a way to destroy it by fire. When you failed to do that you were told to seduce the minister.' The huge woman stood up and shouted, 'How do *you* know that?' She started to advance threateningly, and fast! I raised my hand and said, 'In the Name of Jesus . . .' Her advance stopped as if she had walked into a plate glass window, staggering back to her seat where she remained as if bound, unable to move.

Over the next few weeks she really did change her life. She had come up against the superior power of God and it amazed her, and she became a Christian. She had been a member of a Satanist group which had targeted a particular church in the community for destruction. Yes, it really can happen.

Another church had been split from top to bottom by an insecure pastor who had strongly dominated the congregation. Finally, he had left the church, taking some of the leaders and people with him. Those who were left behind were seriously hurting from much injustice.

A minister was asked to preach for a call to become the next pastor. Before the candidate would preach, he asked permission to pray through the church. The board members, wondering if there might have been a real presence of evil in their church during the previous regime, agreed. The minister prayed until he felt a heaviness leave the sanctuary.

After he had been inducted, two people came to him separately and said, 'You know, pastor, when we came to church the morning you preached for a call, it was like coming into a church filled with light. Before, it used to take us a week to get over being in church so we had strength to come back on Sunday!' The pastor continued to pray every Saturday night in preparation for the Sunday services for the Holy Spirit to cleanse and bless the sanctuary and other parts of the building. Life returned to the gradually healing congregation.

When she was invited by her friend, a woman went out one afternoon to attend a Ladies Guild meeting at her friend's church. It happened to be a fellowship where they had been experiencing serious problems. She went to the main street location where she knew the church stood, but she could not find it. She stood, puzzling how this could be. Then she asked a passer by where the church was. He raised his eyebrows and said, 'It's there. Right behind you!' She turned round to find she had been at the right place all the time, but to her amazement, saw the roof covered with what appeared to be giant slugs! She blinked her eyes, and they were gone. Did this woman see 'in the spirit' the devil's forces at work over an afflicted congregation?

The church has, since earliest times, taken the works of the devil seriously. It is a normal and accepted fact that a church building must be consecrated to the service of God. In the same way that a person is baptized yet is never without the need for prayer and protection, so a church building may be consecrated to the Lord yet remain in need of constant prayer. This is something that the people of God have often forgotten in a materialistic age.

How much of the devil's destroying, robbing, murdering work is focussed on the buildings in which the people of God meet? Just imagine what would happen if every lurking dark spirit, if every demon hanging from the rafters, was beaten out of our sanctuaries, classrooms, offices and corridors! The destroyer's work in creating all kinds of interpersonal problems could be brought to a halt by the right kind of spiritually oriented prayer. Party-spirit, gossip and division of all kinds might be brought to a grinding halt if we only took the need of our buildings for spiritual cleansing and sanctification more seriously.

Sometimes, Satan's robbery of the home and overseas mission-giving of Christ's church might be reversed by appropriate prayers of cleansing and blessing. That murderer's ability to assassinate the innocent character by innuendo and wicked suspicion might be prevented if the leaders of the church prayed through classrooms and hallways as they went about their work for Christ. Both formal and informal prayers are very effective in dealing with institutional problems.

So far, we have been considering church buildings that may

be 'bugged.' Private homes need proper blessing, too. This is another facet of traditional Christianity that has often been thrown out by the church in this sophisticated and secular age.

A family was leaving church one Sunday morning. The father said, 'I wish you would come and speak to our children. We are having terrible trouble with them. They seem to fight about everything. They *believe* in Jesus, but it doesn't seem to make any difference to the way we live.'

I asked the four children, whose ages were between nine and seventeen, 'Do you agree with your Dad?'

They nodded eagerly. 'We do not know why, or what gets into us,' they said.

'How long have you lived in your present house?' I asked the parents.

'About two years,' they replied.

'Did you have this kind of trouble before you moved here?'

'No. We had a peaceful home until we moved to our present place.'

To the whole family I said, 'I suggest you wait till the next time your children are particularly difficult; when they are behaving like hooligans, take them out into the back yard and say something like this (it doesn't matter if you use different words, it's the idea that counts): "*We are a family of Christians and we are speaking in the Name of Jesus Christ, our Lord. We recognize the devil is at work among us, and we therefore bind every evil spirit afflicting us and our house. We command you spirits to leave every part of our property and go to the place prepared for you.*"

'Then go around the perimeter of your lot calling on the Lord to bless it and to let his angels dwell among you. Go inside into the basement and command every demon out of it, then bless it in the name of the Father, Son and Holy Spirit. Do the same thing throughout the house, every room. Pray appropriate blessings over each location as is fitting, such as:

♦ In the kitchen, *"May this room be a place of safety and happiness, where there is always enough food, and words are always under control;"*
♦ In the living room, *"May this always be a room of peace and good fellowship;"*
♦ In the dining room, *"May this place always be a room of good fellowship and generous hospitality;"*
♦ In the bedrooms, *"May this room be a place of good health and healing, of rest and contentment and godly love."*
♦ The bathroom is the most physically dangerous place in the house, and strangely, demons seem to hang around wherever there is water, so pray, *"May this room be a place of personal cleanliness and may all who use it be safe from all harm."*
♦ Then pray for the space above the ceiling and above the house, and for the ground beneath.'

The end of the story is that a week or so passed before a huge fight developed. Father and mother took their three children outside and did what I had suggested, there and inside the house. They never had any more serious trouble. It was over. This was not a case of people making a serious self-assessment. It was not a 'personal improvement' exercise. I have known many families who have gone through a similar process, with success. Sometimes the work has been done privately by one parent because the other was not a Christian, and the children knew nothing about it, either.

There is no need to live in a place that is contaminated by the evil one. When Jesus told us to pray to our Father in heaven, *'deliver us from evil,'* or perhaps a better translation, *'deliver us from the evil one,'* he means that we need not put up with all of Satan's infringement on our lives. The problem is, so often we do not understand where the trouble is coming from. The proof that appropriate prayer works gloriously is in the resulting enhancement of life and liberty.

During a week in which she had stayed with us, we had been able to help Anita with several problems in her new faith as a Christian. She was a rich woman whose third husband's name was Desmond. Their marriage was not being helped by her two teenage daughters who caused continuous strife, and were always fighting. When the March-break followed soon afterwards, she and her husband took their two daughters to the tropics and generously loaned their mansion to us, along with their servants, for the week.

Our two youngest children, Alison and Ian, were still at home in those days, and came with Delphine and me for the holiday. Aged seventeen and sixteen, our two had enjoyed the usual minor childhood spats and tussles but, on the whole, had always been the very best of friends, and still are. They were shown up to the adjoining rooms of the daughters of the house.

While Delphine and I were admiring the view of the gardens from the billiard-room windows, we heard an explosion of anger from upstairs, and the loud voices of our children arguing as we had never heard before. We ran up to find out what was going on.

Alison and Ian were red-faced and obviously very upset with each other. I stopped them in mid-sentence, discerning the root of the problem. 'Be quiet! There are demons in these girls' rooms that are really bothering you. We will get rid of them.' Going into each of the rooms, I prayed in the Name of Jesus and with the authority of his Precious Blood, binding the spirits that infested them, commanding them to leave. Immediately, our children reverted to their normal selves, and continued happily while we stayed in luxury for a memorable holiday.

Two weeks after the March-break, Desmond telephoned. He sounded happier than I had ever heard him. 'David. Whatever did you do while you were here? Ever since we returned home our girls have not had a fight! Even they cannot understand it. Life here is wonderfully different!' So I explained what had happened, and about our prayers to spiritually cleanse the girls' rooms. Desmond was as amazed as he was grateful.

While attending a denominational General Assembly a man approached me. 'I have been told I ought to speak to you. You see, we have a son, Edward, who ran off when he was seventeen and got into the west coast drug scene. He had made a commitment to Christ when he was younger. We did not hear anything from him for many years, then he got in touch with us. A few months ago he turned up on our doorstep and we were just delighted! He moved back in and took over his old bedroom in the basement.

'However, we have had a terrible time since. He has continued with his drugs. We do not know what else he is up to. We can't speak to him. A few days ago he came upstairs and threatened his mother with a knife. He wanted to cut her throat! We had to report him to the police. He has been fairly quiet since then, but we are living in fear and trembling that he will do something terrible to us, or to someone else. He is so full of anger and hatred.'

The son was now thirty years old. When I asked about the man's bedroom, his father said, 'He has painted it all black. On the walls are hideous posters of heavy-metal bands, and evil demon-like things. It is full of confusing colours and patterns. He has his records and books down there. The place is always in a mess. Do you think I should go and destroy all his books and music?'

My suggestion to this greatly troubled Christian father was this: 'Do not touch his property. To do so will only excite his violence needlessly. The best thing you can do is clean up his room spiritually. When your son is out, pray for the Holy Spirit to enable you, then go into his room in the Name of Jesus. Speak as if to the devil, with all the authority of Christ behind you, and tell all demons you are binding them through the power that is in the Precious Blood of Jesus. Tell every spirit to leave the records, the furniture, the books and the very walls, floor and ceiling of the room. Then make a statement to the wider powers of this dark world to the effect: "I am the father of Edward, a man who knows who Christ is and who once received him as Lord of his life. I claim him back for the Kingdom of God and his Son, Jesus Christ. I forbid any more demons to enter this room or to affect my son. Amen." '

Some months later I ran into the man again. He reported joyfully that he had done as I suggested. The result was, his son became much quieter immediately. A few days later he emerged from his room where he usually kept to himself. 'Mum and Dad,' he said. 'I don't know what has been wrong with me for so long now. All I know is, I am so sorry for the trouble I have caused you. Mum, please forgive me for the wicked things I said to you a few weeks ago. Somehow, I think things are going to be better for me from now on.' And they were.

The hospital's nursing administrator was encountering trouble from one person after another. Even other senior members of the staff were saying and doing disruptive and unnecessary things. One night he took me around the corridors, wards and operating rooms. We covered the whole place. As we walked quickly, I prayed and he said 'Amen!'

'Father, we bind and in Jesus' Name command every evil spirit to leave this (ward, office, corridor etc.). We ask you, Lord, to bless the place and the people who work here; let your angels dwell herein and keep it in peace so that your will may be done. Amen!'

The results were immediate. That hospital began to operate better. Goodwill appeared where previously it had been bad. Arguments and self-interest were replaced by accord and civility. The new peace lasted for quite a long time, but, I am sorry to say, reversion slowly took place.

Was this relapse because faithful people did not continue regularly to pray with powerful effect? Did human failure, taking the good for granted, prevent that place of healing from being kept in the liberation that God had shown he wanted? Was it that those who knew about the prayers that had been so effective simply forgot the strength and craftiness of Satan, and presumed upon God's blessing? To take the Lord for granted can be a dangerous thing, indeed.

The cleansing and blessing of buildings occupied by Christians, whether homes, churches or institutions, is a practice with two thousand years of history. If we forget our heritage, today's church stands to lose a lot. The 'spiritual forces of evil' that throng about humanity as we live day by day in this earthly and spiritual realm will laugh and jeer, and continue to cause otherwise avoidable havoc.

Notes

1. 'Testimonies of some former Satanists and cult members would indicate that certain deceived or wicked people are deliberately out to destroy effective Christian ministries.' Anderson, Neill T. and Charles Mylander, *Setting Your Church Free* (Ventura, CA: Regal Books, 1994), 318.
2. ibid.

~ 14 ~

Wisdom Looks Deep

It's a Question of Discernment

The proverb's 'all that glisters is not gold' principle will be applied by the wise Christian to all the experiences that this world provides. Things that appear attractive are not always all they seem to be. Wisdom lies in discerning the true nature of what is observed, sensed, and generally found in the events, conversations, and affairs of every twenty-four-hour period. Only two or three times have I 'seen' an evil spirit as if with my eyes. Careful observation and astute listening to people, however, has often revealed them, and their nature.

Believers, being aware of the ministry of God's angels, must understand that Paul was narrating one of the essential pieces of heavenly revelation when he said, *'Satan himself masquerades as an angel of light'* (2 Cor. 11:14). A young couple worked at a group home for disturbed youths who were there under order of the court. Aware of the great amount of evil and affliction the young people brought into their home, Peter and Robin had been through several experiences with demonic powers. They reached the point where they routinely prayed for their charges with spiritual fervour and delivering effect. Many good things happened from the time they took spiritual warfare seriously.

Though they had a sense that in the invisible realm there was a lot of angry feeling, Peter and Robin were enjoying the first opportunity they had of really helping some of the young people. They began to take deliverance and confrontation with the realm of spiritual evil as a matter of course.

One night, Robin awoke suddenly, in the small hours, to see a beautiful angel at the foot of her bed. She instantly knew that its female beauty was a deception. The 'angel' was hanging upside-down! How did she handle this manifestation, woken by it from the depths of sleep? She knew that she was safe in the hand of God. In her new and godly boldness which had come with the authority of Christ, she said, 'Oh, it's you! Go away! You're through!' She went back to sleep immediately, without fear. Where the Spirit of the Lord is, there is peace. His perfect love casts out all fear.

Discernment can be very helpful, if we understand that we continue to be under the influence of spiritual realities even during the night when we are asleep. During the night, though often we forget the details, we dream. While a mother may fondly wish her child, 'sweet dreams,' she would be an unusual mother not to have experienced being woken in the small hours of the morning by a child's screams.

When a child awakes in terror, it can usually be restored to sleep very quickly by dealing with the nightmare as if it is a demonic affliction. Let the young one receive a blessing in Jesus' Name from his or her mother or father (he will love the reassuring touch of his parent's hand on his head). Follow this with a prayer such as, 'Father, in your glorious Name we plead the Precious Blood of Jesus over [child's name]. We command every evil spirit that has been hurting our child [name] to leave him right now. Bless him now and give him peaceful dreams. Thank you, Lord. Amen.' In all probability, the child will not remember anything about the nightmare in the morning.

Once, a twelve year-old boy came into a storefront drop-in centre. He did not go to church and had no understanding of Christianity. With a Coke and a cookie and a few spare minutes, he sat gladly to hear the story of Jesus and his love. As he was leaving, I asked if there was anything he would like me to pray about for him.

He answered, 'Can you pray about my nightmares? I get the same one again and again. I am always being chased by a man who is going to kill me. It is always the same man, the same story. It seems I always wake up just as he is going to stab me.'

I pleaded the Blood of Christ over the lad and said, 'I command every spirit that causes those bad dreams to leave this boy. God loves him, and the Lord Jesus died for him on the Cross. He wants him to be free of all evil. Amen.'

I never saw the boy at the drop-in centre again, but about two years later, on a Sunday morning, I was standing at the main door of a church in the town where I had been the guest preacher. As I shook hands with people leaving I spotted three young fellows running down the other side of the road. The last of them was my young friend, now grown quite big. He ran over to me, stopped just long enough to give a friendly slap to my outstretched hand, and say, 'Hey, preach! I never had any of those dreams again!' And off he ran!

A child will sometimes complain that there is 'someone' in her or his room, though clearly no one has been there. If this kind of thing happens frequently, it could be that the child is troubled by an evil spirit that haunts the room. Take the possibility that the child is not 'just imagining it' seriously.

In the Name of the Lord Jesus Christ, command the interloper to leave. Once is usually enough to stop the trouble for good.

Fourteen year-old Stephen was at a boarding school where I was the part-time chaplain. He was part of a group preparing for that step in life where they confirm their personal responsibility for being a committed servant of Jesus Christ. One morning I found the school buzzing with the story of Stephen's horrible adventure last night.

The senior boy of Stephen's dormitory had gone round on a final bed-check at about ten o'clock. He was frightened to find the younger boy on his back in bed, struggling to move and unable to breathe, with terror on his face. Somehow, the senior sat him up and slowly the lad returned to some kind of composure.

After classes the following morning, I found Stephen and had him sit with me. He said, 'Sir, it was horrible. I thought I was going to die!' I asked him what happened.

'Well, sir. Yesterday I received a letter from home and my father said my mother had left with another man. I was so shocked. I thought that if *this* was what happened when I was thinking of becoming a real Christian, I wasn't going to go on with it. In fact, I said, "Satan, if you are real, get my mother back."

'Last night, after I had gone to bed, I saw something "foggy" drift cross the room towards me. It came and sat on my chest. It was like a terrible weight and I couldn't breathe. Sir, I think it was Satan. Harris [the senior boy] came in, and rescued me. I did not sleep another wink all night.'

Stephen was ready to ask God to forgive him for praying to Satan. He was certain, now, that he *really* wanted to belong to Jesus! The boy never had any more problems. Since that occasion I have come across other people who have experienced the suffocating power of a dark spirit in a similar way. It is not as uncommon as one might suppose.

The following is also an example of a case of a person who had a serious problem with the devil after he prayed to him. The middle-aged man called me for an appointment. As is my practice, I asked what church he belonged to. (I ask so that, if a person has not already spoken to his pastor about approaching me, he will now do so.) 'I do not go to any church,' he said, 'Someone at work told me to call you.' I listened to his tale briefly, and arranged to see him.

Harry had worked in the same office for more than twenty years, but he had never won the weekly office 'sweep.' Every Friday, like everyone else, he chipped in his twenty-five cents, and every Friday someone else won the kitty. People in the large office used to laugh and jeer at old 'Hopeful Harry.'

It had got beyond a joke, so one day he prayed . . . to the devil . . . that he should win. And he did! The next week, too. And the week following. His chances of winning three times were astronomically remote. Then he won a fourth time in succession, and a fifth.

At this point Harry became really scared. He was now the talk of every person in the office and factory, and even the managers were looking at him strangely! Poor Harry was so scared that he hardly slept now. He had absolutely quit entering the sweep! It was then that someone suggested he get help.

He was *quite* ready to accept the reality of the spirit world. When he learned that he could be set free from the awful grip of the 'luck' that now hung around him like a pall, he was ecstatic. That afternoon, he listened to the Gospel he had heard as a child, and received Christ as Master of his life. He asked for forgiveness for opening his life up to the devil. What a glorious day it turned out to be for him. Harry had learned that the mockery of others need never make him feel worthless again. He had come to grips with greed that in many different ways had simmered within him for so long. Once again, I saw how God could transform a moment of sin into a means of gathering another child into his kingdom.

Once, in Hungary, her home country, a young girl, Maria, was walking home through the forest when she saw a beautiful lady riding on a white horse . . . in the sky! This was the stuff of fairy tales, and she stood, entranced. The apparition came down to ground level and spoke to the child who eagerly accepted the experience as quite wonderful. The fair 'lady' told her that she was the child's angel, and, if she wanted, she would stay close beside her forever, if she would agree to do what she was told. The girl agreed with this wondrous offer.

Forty years later I learned this story from the girl's lips. Maria was by then a widow living in a small home in one of Ontario's agricultural towns, near to us. Throughout her life, during which she had believed in the Son of God, Jesus Christ, she had never lost the beautiful woman's company. The problem was, not long after her experience in the forest, the creature had turned in appearance from female to 'male,' and lost its beauty. But it always remained 'friendly,' insisting that the things it wanted her to do, and the attitudes that it inspired, were religious and good. The woman had always believed that, because Jesus said that each 'little one' has an angel who beholds the face of the Father in heaven, it never occurred to her to doubt that her companion was indeed, an angel from God.

Now she was terribly confused. One day recently, the spirit had presented a plan for the murder of an entire family living a few doors up the road from her. Maria found herself listening to an apparently foolproof design to introduce poison into her neighbour's food. At this, suspicions that had been gathering force in her mind for years became clear.

Maria realized that she had come almost totally to depend for guidance upon an intimate and 'familiar' friend whose advice had often led to broken relationships, and, perhaps, even some of the tragedies that had afflicted her. Now she scarcely knew what to do. She had long since fallen away from attending the Roman Catholic church, and felt nervous about approaching the local priest, so she asked an evangelical pastor to come and visit her.

It was a mid-July day with the temperature in the high 90s Fahrenheit when she told her story to the good man. He looked bewildered. Then he proclaimed that Maria should go and see her doctor. Perhaps she needed to have a 'rest.'

'After all, we do not really believe, today, in demons, do we?' he said.

Whereupon, to the man's shock, the temperature in that very hot and stuffy little front room instantaneously dropped to freezing! The poor fellow was so agitated that he fled the house. He refused to talk to Maria again.

Maria told me her story. She was now seriously doubting if the 'beautiful lady' had ever been an angel of God. I responded by giving her some teaching about the true ways of God, and about the ways in which the arch-deceiver and his messengers work.

As she looked back on all the trouble that had been in her life, she became ready to confess that it might really have been a deceiving spirit all the time, sent to ruin her. She had honestly thought, down through the years, that the apparition had been sent by God to try her, an instrument for strengthening her faith in God. Of course, it had been sent by the enemy to strengthen her faith in the anti-Christ (opposite-to-Christ) spirit.

After she had sobbed out appropriate prayers of repentance, the gentle-hearted Maria surrendered herself to Jesus as Lord of her life. Prayers of deliverance set her free at last from the demon that had plagued her for so long. A few months later, she was enjoying her life as never before, but she had not wanted to go to the church to which I had introduced her. She did not participate in the life of the body of Christ and receive much needed discipleship training, Holy Communion and teaching from the Scriptures.

The following winter I happened to be in her town so I called to speak to her. She welcomed me nervously with a wry smile which was new. Then she told me:

'I was sitting here one night watching the television when, all of a sudden, I heard the voice of the spirit very clearly. "Please let me speak to you. I will be good. I miss you so much!" I turned off the television and said, "No! I don't want anything to do with you ever again!"'

Maria continued, 'Then I found myself in conversation with it. Before I knew what was happening, I discovered I was feeling sorry for the spirit. It said that ever since the deliverance it had been outside in the cold, all alone, and how would I like to be outside in the cold all alone? Couldn't it at least show itself to me so that it could explain how it had changed its ways, like I had?'

'So I let it show me itself. I felt so sorry for it. It was like an old friend. I let it stay, and it has been with me ever since!'

The spirit was keeping a low profile. It had not promoted any evil, said it had only been joking when it suggested the murder of the neighbouring family, and protested that if it stayed long enough, it too might be 'saved,' as Maria had been!

Poor Maria. She had been so lonely that the idea of having someone familiar in her life again had been too much to resist. She would not listen to me when I tried to obtain her release this time. She was stubbornly earnest in her protestation that the spirit would not now harm her. All my arguments fell on deaf ears. She would not accept that she had let in a creature which would increasingly worm its way into her confidence, trying slowly to take over the ruling right and primacy of Christ. I never saw her again, but have often wondered how she who was lost, then found and set free, could have allowed her natural feelings of sympathy and loneliness to outrank the obedience and love of the Lord she had so joyfully come to know.

I do not think Maria's case an example of what Jesus had in mind when he said, '*When an evil spirit comes out of a man, it goes through arid places seeking rest and does not find it. Then it says, "I will return to the house I left." When it arrives, it finds the house swept clean and put in order. Then it goes and takes seven other spirits more wicked than itself, and they go in and live there. And the final condition of that man is worse than the first*' (Luke 11:24-26).

I feel certain that when spirits are bound in Christ's name and sent away 'to the place prepared for them' (in the words of an ancient prayer of exorcism), they go to a place where they are bound to remain forever. I have heard, on occasion, demons speak in fear or resignation about this fate. Once I 'saw' a demon tumbling down what seemed to be a long, dark tunnel and heard the failing echo of its cries. There was a sense of finality about its end.

However, a communications 'Internet' exists in the realm

of Satan. This means that another spirit can be called into service to replace one dismissed in the name of the Lord Jesus Christ.

Demons are known to change their appearance and voices, and are good at deceptive disguise. I feel convinced that the spirit that came to deceive Maria after she had been set free from the one she had entertained for many years was another creature, sent to work away at a weakness which was on record.

Another facet of this evil 'follow-up' kind of spiritual warfare is what I call 'the echo.' People who have been demonized sometimes, very soon after deliverance, experience temptation in the moral area from which they have been spiritually delivered. The person gloriously liberated will now be able to sense with the returning temptation a spiritual element. Perhaps there might be audible or grossly obviously demonic attempts to cause another downfall. However, the temptation to the soul is not as overpowering as it used to be. I call this an 'echo from outer darkness.'

The 'echo' is as if the departed demon spitefully calls back to its victim. It cannot resist trying to persuade its old host that true and full deliverance did not really happen. People who are taught properly, on hearing this 'echo' simply stand firm and tell the spirit that they are eternally free from the old problem, that they have been liberated by the grace of the Lord Jesus Christ, and they cannot be harmed again in that way. The problem diminishes immediately, or disappears totally.

Realising the reality of the spirit world can be of enormous help for all Christians who are serious about taking up their cross and following Jesus, pursuing the way of holiness. Our Lord contended with Satan himself throughout his life and wanted us to pray, *'Deliver us from evil.'*

~ 15 ~

Words Have Power – Believe It!

Receive Blessings – Counter Curses

'Pastor, I have never told you this before, but you once said something that has totally changed my life! I always used to be full of doubts. I understood what the Bible was saying, but, even though I really wanted to believe, doubts kept flooding my mind.

'You may not remember what you said to me, so I will tell you what it was. You said, "Tommy, the answer for you is very simple. The next time you find a doubt surging up in your mind, *tell it to go away, in the name of the Lord Jesus Christ!* You have probably been affected by a spirit, or spirits of doubt. All demons are subject to the word of God. Just deal with doubt like that." I shrugged my shoulders . . . and wondered. I respected you as a pastor, but . . . well . . .

'I want to tell you now that I did exactly what you said with the next doubt about Christ or the Bible that shot into my mind, *and it WENT!* Just like that! It was gone. I was amazed! I had to do it a few times as the days went by, and then, all my doubts had gone. I never have any trouble at all now. I believe the Scriptures and the teaching. I don't *understand* it all, but I *believe* it. I never knew Christianity could be so exciting.'

The truth is, 'we can have what we say' (Mark 11:23).

Doubt is one of those 'mountains' that Jesus was talking about which can be commanded, *'Go, throw yourself into the sea!'* For the Jews, the sea represented something terrible and chaotic, just the place for discarded problems, like doubt. I take Christ's graphic, maritime illustration to be a poetic way of describing an authoritative charge to our 'mountain' meaning 'get lost – permanently!' *'The sea'* need not be taken literally, I think.

Tommy had discovered the practical reality of the power of the tongue. The Bible attests repeatedly that the lips, the tongue, are instruments both for good and for evil. Christ our Lord judged the use to which people put their tongues, very severely. *'But I tell you that men will have to give account on the day of judgment for every careless word they have spoken. For by your words you will be acquitted, and by your words you will be condemned'* (Matt. 12:36,37).

James spoke of the difficulty people find with taming the tongue. *'With the tongue we praise our Lord and Father, and with it we curse men, who have been made in God's likeness'* (James 3:9). Satan exerts a lot of influence against humanity and the purposes of God through the access he so easily gains to human words. The power of speech is one of the characteristics which distinguishes human beings from all the rest of this world's creation and is a proof that we are made in God's image. It is, therefore, most hated by the enemy of our souls. If he can corrupt it, he will.

The reason our tongues, our lips, are such a focal point for the devil is not hard to find. The Son of God is the living Word of God. When people become God's children through faith in Jesus Christ (John 1:12) they receive the Holy Spirit, the very Spirit of the living God, the Spirit of Jesus. His words are always gracious and *very* powerful. He desires to use our lips to speak to the world for him, to *'make disciples of all nations ... teaching them to obey everything [he has] commanded'* (Matt. 28:19,20). If Satan can get hold of a person's tongue and use it in forbidden ways (by causing party-spirit, division, distrust and suspicion; by cursing, backbiting, complaining, lying, cheating, defaming, slandering, destructive criticism, for example) then he laughs at us.

The devil has the right to mock any Christian who professes to believe in Jesus and yet whose words characterize someone who is an agent of the devil. Christians (I have known some) who have a good knowledge of Christian doctrine, a swift readiness to quote the Bible, and sometimes a position of leadership and influence in a church, but who spend time talking about this person or that to a third party, had better beware. They are typical of just the sort of soul Satan infiltrates to wreak dissension and confusion in the church.

When someone has a genuine grievance against another, the right person to speak to is the one who causes the grief, not someone else. The teaching of Christ, in Matthew 18:15-17, is very clear. To get on the phone to a 'friend' and complain about another person, is to play right into the devil's hands and to damage one's own soul, as well as cause subtle harm to the 'friend.' To gossip is not reproducing the character of Christ. It is sin!

If someone still finds that she or he has a great urge to talk like this after heartfelt confession of the sin of it, she or he may need deliverance. The damnable forces of destruction in Christian churches can be very subtle and self-righteous. Too many ears are ready to be oiled by complaints and scandals. But like every other sin, except blasphemy against the Holy Spirit, such sins *may* be forgiven, *if* they are repented of. James 3:6 warns Christians to be aware that their tongues can easily be set on fire by hell.

On the other hand, blessings from a believer's lips have great power to do good. I once read of a person undergoing deliverance who asked for a drink of water. She still possessed several demons when her minister gave her the glass 'in the Name of the Lord Jesus Christ.' She vomited the water. This happened several times until he gave her water without the blessing. That she swallowed and kept down. The devil knows the difference that a blessing can make: I wonder if church people do?

The blessings that come from the sincere person's tongue to his or her spouse or children have real effect. Many well-balanced people, successful with living, have been positively affirmed and frequently blessed verbally by their parents. On the other hand, the curses that fall from idle or angry lips have destructive effect. Many people who have confessed low self-esteem to me have often experienced repeatedly the damning curses of their parents: 'You are stupid!' 'You will never come to anything!' 'You are lazy, always lazy!' 'You are just like your father ... (a dead loss!).' 'You are always [this or that negative characteristic].'

An afflicted person must come to terms with the need to grant forgiveness to the offensive relative, for Christ's sake. Then, as experience shows, treating such curses as if they have demonic origin can lead to renunciation of the evil spirits that lay behind the curses ('stupidity' for example). A person can be set free from the related stigma and inspired into a new and vigorously different life.

Though confession and receiving forgiveness are essential steps in gaining spiritual liberty, it is often only at the words of deliverance that real release becomes fully experienced.

'Something *happened*!' a person might say. A smile spreads across the face; 'I feel all *clean* inside!' or, 'The voices have gone!'

The following account is an example of a profound difference which was immediately perceived after deliverance prayers. It concerns the power of a curse being met by the power of the Holy Spirit.

Michelle hailed from Quebec and was a member of a large family. Brought up religiously, she had heard the Gospel read Sunday by Sunday all her life, but had never learned the need to take the step of putting her full personal trust in God. After she came to a personal acceptance of the sacrifice of Christ for her sins, Michelle became a dynamic Christian.

Among all her brothers and sisters, her elder brother, Jacques, was often the subject of her prayers. How she wanted him to be blessed! But Jacques was a violent man, often in trouble with the law, and now he seemed to have disappeared altogether. As I heard her story, I was very interested and said to Michelle, 'If he ever comes around here, I'd like to meet him.'

One afternoon a year or so later, the phone rang. Michelle's close friend Jeanette was on the line. She sounded urgent. 'I am at Michelle's. She says I'm to tell you "Jacques is here."' I felt a pang of concern at the edge in her voice because I feared he could be violent.

Soon, I arrived at Michelle's door, knocked, and walked in. The two women were sitting with their hands in their laps, eyes wide, as Jacques, in a workman's dirty shirt and pants, obviously drunk, alternatively shouted and muttered in French and in English. I went straight into the action I knew best. 'Jacques, I am David Mitchell, a minister of the

Lord Jesus Christ. I have been looking forward to meeting you!' I reached out my hand, to which he responded gently with his own which was huge, rough, and very powerful. He muttered something.

Michelle said, 'The police brought him here. He was staying overnight in a hotel in [she named a nearby village] and a man attacked him. He hit the man so hard he fractured his skull, but the police say it was self-defence, so they are not laying charges. He had no money and they managed to learn that his sister lived not far away, and here he is.'

I began to question Jacques, to talk about Jesus Christ, and what he can do for someone whose life is in chaos. But it was no use. He was as drunk as a newt! I said to the women, 'I'm sorry. I can't do anything while he is like this. Give me a call when he is sober.'

I started to get up to leave but, before our eyes, in a flash, Jacques sobered up! We were astonished. Even the smell of drink seemed to have gone. We knew this could only be the hand of God.

Soon Jacques was telling his life's story. It was a history of violence of every kind from the time he was a young man. On his brawny arms I noticed a series of round-shaped scars, including some recent ones. 'How did you get these scars, Jacques?' I enquired quietly.

'I get them all the time. That's how I get money. I let people stub out their smokes in my arms, ten bucks for a cigarette, twenty-five for a cigar!'

'Is that the only way you earn a living?' I asked.

'Oh, no! I am a professional arm-wrestler. I have never been beaten, and I have never lost a fight!' His chest swelled at his prowess. He looked at his sister for confirmation. Michelle nodded.

I still found that hard to believe, so I asked, 'How is that possible?'

Jacques spoke rapidly, as if he wanted to get this part of the conversation over. 'When my grandfather was dying, he reached out and said, "Jacques, I give you my strong right hand!" And then he died.'

I said, 'Jacques, that was not a blessing, that was a curse!'

Jacques looked steadily into my eyes, paused, and said, 'Yes, I know.'

My question to him was, 'Would you like to be rid of that curse?'

'Yes, I would. It has got me into much trouble. I always win my fights, but I always get hurt, too. People are always challenging me to a fight and I have to do it. I would like to get rid of the curse.'

I explained that Jesus Christ came into the world to bless God's children, all who believe in him. If Jacques surrendered his life to Christ, he would bless him and then we could use his authority to rid him from his grandfather's curse. Quickly the man fell upon his knees and made a heartfelt confession of faith and of sins committed down the years. He wept. Michelle and Jeanette wept, too.

When he was composed and comfortable in an armchair, I said, 'Now let us rid you of the curse.' I continued, 'If you could see the Lord Jesus right now, would you put your hand in his?' Jacques nodded vigorously.

'Well, we cannot see him, but he is here. Use my hand as if it were his, put your hand in it and say, "Lord Jesus, I give you my strong right hand. Take the curse of my grandfather away."' Jacques did as I suggested with firm and definite purpose.

Then, the words said, he shook himself, looked at me

135

strangely, and said, 'What have you done? What have you done? Here! You arm wrestle with me!' He prepared to get down by the coffee table, rolling his sleeves right up so I could see huge, bulging muscles.

I laughed, nervously. 'Listen, Jacques, the strongest thing I have to do is push a pencil,' I said. Then I thought, or rather prayed silently, 'Dear Lord, you are the God of power and might. I have been obedient to you in this matter. Will *you* show Jacques that you are the mighty one, so that he can really trust you from now on.'

To Jacques I said, 'Jacques, you can see that I am no match for a man who has never lost an arm-wrestling match, but my God will show you that *he* is stronger than any man's arm.' With that, I rolled up my right sleeve and put my elbow on the table. His great fist swallowed mine!

Jacques smiled. I used no strength of my own. It seemed as if my hand was resting lightly against a wall of steel. The other side of that steel, Jacques pushed and shoved. The veins stood out on his forehead. His body twisted with great force. The torque must have been tremendous. He sweated and strained, and my hand rested lightly against the invisible wall.

Then, I felt certain the Lord was saying, 'Now show him where real strength comes from, David.' I pushed against that steel wall ever . . . so . . . slightly, and Jacques was flung violently backwards as if by a giant. The first time in his life, he was beaten in a trial of strength.

Jacques stayed around a few days, a different brother to the one Michelle had always known. He seemed very happy. Then, just as quickly as he had appeared, he left on his travels again, but this time he was not accompanied by the spirit of his grandfather's curse, but by the Spirit of Jesus.

Illness may be caused by a curse. Freda and Hugh made

an unscheduled return from a far eastern mission field where they had worked together for half a lifetime. Freda had become very ill, and nothing could be done for her overseas. The problem was that despite excellent service from highly qualified medical advisors in Canada, still nothing could be done for her.

At the suggestion of their mission chief, Freda and Hugh approached me while we happened to be attending the same conference. I listened carefully to her story. Clearly, as all medical or psychological causes had already been investigated thoroughly, I began to look for possible openings in the spiritual realm, for demonic influence. All my questions proved to me that, beyond any shadow of doubt, Freda was a holy woman, free from any overt sin or occult interest.

As her story unfolded, a particular relationship appeared to have caused her a great deal of trouble. A native woman, the head of the church's work in a particular village, had become aggressive and rebellious to authority. The missionaries began to wonder at her manipulative and, though they hated to say it, pagan ways.

Then, one day she had come with another woman to the mission house. Entering the yard she had begun to shout and scream, uttering terrible curses on Freda, who responded with shock and disbelief.

As she related the story, Freda began to realize that her sickness had come upon her from that time. Was this just a coincidence?

My question to Freda was, 'How did you receive this curse? Did you immediately respond in your heart and in words, such as, *"I am a Christian: I am washed in the Blood of Jesus Christ: I belong to God: and I resist the curse in Jesus' name. I do not receive it. I cast it back to its source, even the enemy of God and of humankind! AMEN!"* Or did you back away in fear, and allow doubt and horror to engulf you?'

Freda looked shamefaced. 'I did not know what to do. I was so shaken, I responded in the second way. Oh, if only I had been taught how to deal with such things! We were taught nothing about dealing with demons.'

At issue was the reason why the curse had been able to 'stick' to a saint. When I pointed out how it had occurred, Freda was quick to acknowledge that the cause was *sin*. The problem was, *she had responded as if the power of the curse was greater than the power of Jesus Christ, her Lord.*

I said to her, 'In a sense, Freda, you were reduced to honouring the cursing woman more than the blessed Christ. The Lord has allowed you to pay a consequence of what was, in fact, idolatry. As soon as anything, or anyone, becomes more significant to us than God, we are guilty of that sin. We break the cardinal commandment.' Freda felt instantly convicted of the sin. Quickly, she was ready to kneel and confess to the Lord that she had been crushed by fear when all the time his perfect love was already within her heart, more than sufficient to drive all fear out. She was astonished that she could so easily have fallen for the enemy's trick. How she regretted allowing that moment of surprise, when the woman had burst into her front yard, to catch her spiritually unawares. Freda received forgiveness from our gentle Lord who understands how hard it is for his children to be as discerning as they should be.

Next followed prayers of deliverance from the spirits that had come upon Freda in her moment of weakness, including every spirit of disease. She was *forthwith* healed, and quickly returned triumphantly with her husband to the field where they began teaching and ministering in spiritual warfare!

Curses do not always come with a 'Fanfare' like Freda's. A curse can come on one unnoticed, as happened when Alice, a young bride, was told by a man who was a guest at her wedding, 'You will have trouble with Bill. He is a ladies' man.'

Sixteen years later, Bill and Alice had become close personal friends of my wife Delphine and me. Then one day, Bill confessed that Alice was giving him a very rough time. She was accusing him of being with other women. Not only had she started accusing him of being with some of the female staff at his business whenever he was on the evening shift, but now he only had to go out to the town shops on Saturday to find accusation and tears waiting for him when he returned.

Alice was not reluctant to talk about her suspicions to me and Delphine. When I tried to reason with her, and gave specific examples of the falseness of her suspicions regarding occasions when Bill and I had been together, she still was left with a terrible doubt.

It was when I began to ask questions about the origin of her anxieties that she remembered the long forgotten words of the wedding guest. She did not understand that what was said that day was a curse that had entered her soul. It had sown the distress that was now culminating so seriously that it threatened her marriage. She was rapidly becoming impossible to live with.

Alice had become a Christian in recent years and was ready to acknowledge that she had allowed the malicious and unjustified comments of the guest to count more heavily in her mind than the years of faithful marriage Bill had given her. She had not recognized the devilish power behind the man's words. Neither had she known how to deal with her suspicions in a godly fashion.

139

Alice asked for Bill's forgiveness, which was readily given. She renounced the spirits behind the curse in the name of Jesus Christ, and was instantaneously and totally set free from a frame of mind and attitude which had been deteriorating for sixteen years. What a mighty blessing!

Doctor Douglas was nearing the end of his career as an honoured theologian and church administrator. One day, he confessed to me, 'Though I was once a missionary to China, and in more recent years have entered into a very deep personal relationship with Jesus Christ and the Holy Spirit, I have never led anyone to the Lord. Why is this? I have always wanted to see people come to personal faith in Jesus.'

We talked, and I listened to his interesting history. Douglas had two years in China before the communists took over in 1949. During that time he had been learning the language. I found myself asking him, 'Douglas, did you ever enter a Chinese temple, or attend non-Christian ceremonies without pleading the Precious Blood of Christ over yourself first?'

'David,' he answered, 'Yes, I did go into a temple. I was inquisitive. I did not know anything about the notion of pleading the Blood in those days. I remember a man standing by a big brass gong at the entrance. He gave me such a glare! I admit that I felt nervous.'

'Douglas,' I said, 'Curiosity got us into the whole mess we are in! Adam and Eve were curious to know about sin! A Christian may with safety go anywhere, even into the darkest of places or the most wicked of situations, providing he goes in for the right reason, and with a sense of the blessing of God. Right reasons might include going to minister in Christ's name within the place or circumstances, or to learn how to minister with appropriate understanding. You could have gone safely into that temple if it was so that you could speak with knowledge to people who worship in such a place. In that case, your visit could have been made under the protection of the Almighty, but to go out of mere curiosity invited trouble.'

Just as I finished speaking, I had a clear mental picture of Douglas passing the man at the temple entrance. Two Chinese-sounding words came to my mind (the only Chinese I know is 'Beijing,' 'Hong Kong' and other place names!). I said the words out loud to Douglas, who felt he should straightway confess his sin. He renounced spirits named by those two words, and experienced sudden relief in his soul.

Twenty years later I was the mentor to a Chinese man, a scholar, as he was preparing for ordination. I remembered those two 'Chinese-sounding words' and, somewhat self-consciously, asked him if they meant anything. 'Oh yes,' he replied, 'They mean *"Spirit of China."* '

Had my friend Douglas suffered defeat in his evangelistic ministry for so many years, because of mere curiosity? Could that frightening man at the temple entrance have brought a curse upon him because he had never been taught about spiritual danger?

Curses can come with devastating effect. I once counselled a seminary student who had been a successful church planter. He had returned to the seminary as a means of returning to pastoral ministry, after having been out in the secular workplace for about ten years. He did not know why his ministry had failed. I probed until I found what seemed to me to be the cause of his downfall. His story follows:

'I was planting a church in Western Canada, and it was growing fast. We had a great congregation. One day, I knocked on a door and introduced myself. The man invited me in. He was quite receptive to my approach. Suddenly his wife entered the room. When she heard who I was, she began to shout and scream! Then, to my astonishment, she jumped up on the table and continued to bring down a stream of curses on Christ, the church and me. I stammered my apologies to the man, and left.'

From that time onwards the new church began to fail, and a godly young minister who had not been trained how to recognize a demonic attack, and did not know how defend himself spiritually, lost ten years of service to the cause of Christ.

Yes, I believe with the Scripture, *'The tongue has the power of life and death'* (Prov. 18:21). Christians have the blessed power to bring great good into the lives of their family, friends and acquaintances. It will, I fear, be a terrible shock for some Christians to hear the judgment of Christ upon their 'careless words,' or, worse still, their curses.

~ 16 ~

It Is Not Only Your Bright Blue Eyes...!

Dealing with Inherited Demons

It is not only your bright blue eyes, or your brown hair, or your freckles that you inherit from your ancestors. We inherit many of our attitudes and propensities, aptitudes and dispositions. Character can be seen flowing from one generation to the next. It is a wonder to meet whole families which, generation after generation, have followed Jesus Christ as Lord. Children have been brought up in the fear and love of God and each, in his or her turn, has embraced the faith.

They grew up in the presence of the Holy Spirit who indwelt their parents and grandparents before them. Those children were under the good influence of the Spirit of God and, at some time in their lives, welcomed him into their hearts. They identified with Jesus and, either as a process or in a particular moment, accepted his lordship.

Similarly, children can be born into families where the evil spirit is master. There they are surrounded by parents and relatives who set bad examples. They have an inheritance of evil. When a parent is a person in whom an evil spirit is active, and when demonic forces are present in the home, children can be so affected that they identify sufficiently with the evil to 'pick up' spirits from their parents.

Because of many people I have interviewed, I am also

143

convinced that sometimes evil spirits flow into an infant, probably even from before birth. This is particularly observable in women who have 'gifts' of clairvoyance or who are spirit mediums. They will look back on life and know that there has never been a time they can remember that they did not have the 'gift.'

The hearing of voices is another phenomenon which can date from the earliest memories. A man, recently recommitted to Christ, who had heard voices inside his head since infancy, had inherited a particularly violent temper. One day he punched a hole through the double-glazed window of the front door because his wife had locked him out. He had chased her with a knife, threatening her life, not for the first time.

When his pastor introduced me to Hector, I quickly found out about his 'voices.' It was clear that he was extremely penitent about his violent nature. Without preliminaries I asked him to say, '*In the Name of the Lord Jesus Christ, I plead his Precious Blood between me and all my ancestors. I claim the power of the Cross between me and them. I turn back every curse that has come upon me.*' His pastor and I looked on in wonder as a beautiful smile spread across his face. We sat silently for a full minute. Then his pastor said, 'Can you tell us about it, Hector?'

He looked up from his reverie, and said, 'This is the first time in my life I have ever been without voices. Oh, praise the Lord!' By that simple breaking with his father and the long line before him, Hector was healed of his outrageous temper.

Another form of spiritual evil which goes from generation to generation is the spirit of manipulation. It seeks out both men and women, as I shall illustrate.

A related spirit is 'witchcraft' which is also a supremely manipulative spirit. Witchcraft is concerned with controlling nature, circumstances and people so that the perpetrator can have her, or his own way.

As an example, consider a daughter who, in middle age, is still being given a hellish life by her interfering, controlling mother. She stands a good chance of proving to be the same kind of mother to her own daughter. This is partly learned behaviour, of course.

The demonic element can be discovered in the middle-aged woman. She hates the overpowering influence her mother continues to exert on her. At the same time, she hates the way that she finds it almost impossible to stop repeating the same behaviour with her own adult child. She does not know what to do about it. It seems to be beyond her ability to change either relationship. She is imprisoned by them.

As with all deliverance, the question of sin has to be dealt with first. The desire of the manipulator is to be as a god, a know-all kind of god who insists, 'I will have *my* way,' '*I* know best,' 'I want to know *what* you are doing, *when* you are doing it, and *who with!*' This is nothing less than a determination to replace the Lord God Almighty in the daughter's life, a Lord who is not at all like the manipulating counterfeit. I have observed that this evil spirit *may* occur in ostensibly Christian women (well, at least, they can be churchgoing, 'religious' folk!).

Naturally, this kind of influence can destroy a marriage. No area of life may be kept personal or private from the meddler. Grandchildren can be subjected to cloying 'love' which often portrays the grandmother as one who *really* understands, much better than the child's mother, of course.

Often, the first step in obtaining release from these cunning and destructive forms of demonization is for the daughter to face honestly, for the first time in her life, what she has never dared face before – that her mother, in this respect, is a wicked woman! To be honest about her feelings toward her parent can be the first vital step toward obtaining deliverance from her. When the truth is received by a woman for herself, she can be released from the demonic bondage. Then the release of the whole family can follow. Her marriage can be set on a new course. The joyful liberty that belongs to her, her husband and children can begin to illuminate their lives, set free by Christ.

The love of Christ, now set free in the daughter, will often affect the manipulating mother, sometimes to the point when she herself becomes willing for deliverance. Then it is that the counsellor learns that *her* mother was a woman of the same sort, and her grandmother before that.

The wise reader will allow that a man who falls in love with a woman still under the manipulative hand of her mother had better be very careful! He has a very serious potential problem, however much he loves her. Possible calamity can only be averted by the grace of God and a wholehearted willingness of his sweetheart to submit her relationship with her mother to the intense love and power of Christ. No man can play the Scriptural role of a husband if his mother-in-law retains first place in his wife's mind.

To show evil inheritance on the male side, I will speak of Joe. He was a man with a past. He had been brought up in New York, a member of a Mafia family. As a son he had been taught his trade of violence, blackmail, extortion, prostitution, and even murder. Then Joe was converted from merely nominal 'religion' and from his way of life. He became a wholehearted servant of the Lord Christ. He was married to a beautiful Christian lady and had four delightful children.

One day, Joe called me long-distance. 'David, we are having trouble with our eldest boy, Joey. The doctors can't do anything for him, and neither can our pastor. I hardly like to bother you, but we are desperate. He is fourteen now, but he is behaving worse than an infant.' Joe's voice faltered.

'Well, Joe. Tell me. What is he doing that is causing so much difficulty?' I asked.

'David,' he replied, 'this is very hard for me. You know I am still a proud man! He's taken to relieving himself in his closet! He refuses to use the toilet. He shuts himself in his closet and does his business!'

Well! That was a new one for me. I thought I had heard just about every kind of human aberration. Over the telephone, I questioned Joe, but there was not much to add to what I already knew about the family. I quickly had to pray silently in the Spirit to the Lord for specific guidance.

I found my imagination looking at furniture in the boy's bedroom. 'Joe,' I said. 'Tell me about the furniture Joey has in his bedroom.'

'What a strange question, David! It's furniture I had as a kid.' Then, it was as if a light went on in Joe's mind. 'You don't think Joey's trouble is connected with the *furniture*, do you? Oh . . . Come on!'

I answered, 'Joe. I don't want you to tell your wife, Joey, or anyone else what you are now going to do. I believe the Lord has shown me that some of the unclean spirits which were common in your family have stuck to the furniture. Satan is mad at you for leaving him. In his spite he wants to harm your son. He would like to give Joey a foul problem that would lead to him eventually being taken away into an institution. But you have authority, in the Name of Jesus Christ, to deal with this serious matter. I will pray with you first, then you must go into his bedroom when no one is around, and say something like this: *'Every evil and unclean spirit that came with this furniture, from my family, hear me! I am Joe [family name] and I am a Christian, washed in the Blood of the Lord Jesus Christ. By his authority and the power of his Blood shed for my son, Joey [family name], I bind you, and I command you to leave this furniture and my son, and go to the place prepared for you! AMEN.'*

I prayed with Joe, and he did what I suggested, not speaking of it to anyone. Immediately his son was back to normal. Sometime later, his father explained all that had happened, and the family all gave the glory to God!

The question of spiritual inheritance, both good and evil, cannot be discussed without referring to the second Commandment. In it God says that to worship other gods is to cause God to respond with severity toward the worshipper's children, to the fourth generation: *'For I, the Lord your God, am a jealous God, punishing the children for the sin of their fathers to the third and fourth generation of those who hate me, but showing love to thousands who love me and keep my commandments'* (Exod. 20:5-6).

We have seen how blessed families can be by the faith and obedience of their forefathers. In this chapter, and previously when I mentioned the inheritance of occult spirits of divination, we have acknowledged how cursed people can be by their ancestors' rebellion against the loving-kindness of God.

One of the inheritances of evil that I have seen repeatedly is that which flows from a wicked, incestuous father. The man who uses his daughter for sexual reasons must be of all

148

men most vile. When I have talked with such people after their conversion, they have always been the sons of similarly immoral men.

The problem which stems from this wickedness affects their girl children very seriously. Often, they have been subjected to molesting, even from grandfathers, from a very early age. Worse cases still emerge where very young children have been continuously forced to submit to sexual intercourse. In one family of girls, all were forced to give themselves to the service of their father and his friends. They became inured to the suffering, sometimes feeling guilty for their desire to reject their father because to do so would cause him to be unhappy, and this would mean misery for the whole family! This, surely, is manipulation of the most wicked sort.

Girls who are treated incestuously by their father, and often by their brother, too, are fixed with a spirit of self-hatred, which is the origin of so much 'low self-esteem' that one has witnessed. As they grow older, typically such young women often fall into the trap of believing that the only way they can feel loved, worthwhile, is by giving sexual favours to men. They are picked up easily by the wrong kind of boys at high school, and have affairs with men, single or married, it does not matter.

Usually, it seems to me, a woman with this type of history will tend to be self-destructive. Scars on her wrists tell of times she has harmed herself. She may take drug overdoses in the hope of ending her life. Every prostitute I have met has had a history of sexual abuse as a child.

Satan is narrow-minded, repetitious and mechanistic. His ways are reproduced in countless lives. A skilled counsellor can often be assured that if one sinful/demonic characteristic appears in a life, other related ones will be there too.

A woman who has been subjected to sexual abuse as a child will take the effects into her adult life, whether married or single, whether a believer or not, until the fact of sin against her is dealt with. Parallel with the sins inflicted upon her will be her own personal sin, and this is often the missing key to effecting total deliverance and new life for such a woman.

How can a person be said to sin, if the wickedness was from outside and was not generated within her? Quite simply, *she began to sin the moment she thought that she was of little or no worth.*

The truth is, she was known and loved by God before the foundation of the world (Rev. 13:8b). She was in the mind of God when the Triune God planned the redemption of the world before ever Creation came into being (Rev. 17:8). He knew that she would one day believe in Jesus Christ and be reborn of the Spirit (Eph. 1:4-5). What a sin it was (though how natural in the circumstances of penetrating evil) to believe contrary to God's word. Yet how could a little child know God's word unless she had been taught? And so the girl was entrapped, as Satan hoped, for life and eternity. But one day she received the Gospel truth about Jesus' love for her, and the forgiveness of sins, and began on the way of salvation.

The problem was, however, that no one told her that she had probably inherited demonic influences which manifest themselves in such ways as seemingly inescapable 'self-pity.' Though knowing the love of God now, 'self-hatred' also lurks. 'Suicide' may still continue to offer a hideous escape. If still single, the woman may find that she cannot resist the sexual advances of any man on a date. She is still hooked by a 'Whore' spirit.

Should the woman now be married, the couple may find that sexual satisfaction becomes almost impossible. The woman might withhold herself from her husband, not because she is unloving, but ... well ... she does not really know why! One of the stratagems of Satan in a case like this is so to frustrate the husband that he might yield to the temptation to force himself upon his wife, and that could be the beginning of the end of their marriage.

Repeatedly I have found that women such as I have described may be set free for single or married life, 'in all its fullness,' when they have brought their afflictions to the Cross of Christ and have followed this with prayers of renunciation and deliverance.

One of the hardest elements to break is that of demonic control which the father exercised. Before all else, the woman needs honestly to recognize the repugnancy of her father's behaviour, and how abhorrent it was to God. This is particularly difficult when the father was a 'Christian.' If the man was a believer, he could have been from any part of the church, traditional, evangelical, fundamentalist, or any of the 'Bible-believing' sects, I have known them all.

None of these problems are insurmountable. Confession, renunciation and the authoritative prayer of deliverance in the Name of the Lord Jesus Christ will bring liberty and joy as may not have been imagined. Both daughters and fathers can be saved from their situations, but a willingness to be absolutely honest and to submit to the rule and authority of God and the Holy Scripture is essential.

~ 17 ~

One Man's Sorcery is Another Man's Smoke
The Devil and Tobacco (and Other Drugs)

iddle-aged Sarah had been in sexual bondage to her father since infancy. The day she was delivered from this dreadful condition she recounted some of her long periods in various psychiatric hospitals. When she came into the liberty that was her right as a child of God, Sarah was out on a weekly pass from her present institution. On an earlier occasion, while spending six months inside under lock and key and various drug therapies, she had been so bored with nothing to do all day that she had started smoking. She thought to herself at the time, 'I will stop as soon as I get out.' Since then she had tried every legitimate means to rid herself of her habit, without any success.

On deliverance day, several years later, she mentioned her problem. Now, we realize that the smoking habit may be a simple physical addiction, in most cases. But I have learned that sometimes it can have a demon at its root. It must be exorcized before freedom from the habit can be received. On this occasion, because Sarah had shown that there was demonic bondage already present, we thought it worth considering that her smoking trouble might also be a demonic one. We bound the spirits of Tobacco, Smoking and Nicotine (the smoking spirit may hide behind any such name).

As she left, I forgot to give Sarah my usual advice, 'The only cigarette you do not have to smoke is the next one!' So, next day I spoke to her to find out how she had got on. 'I have only tried to smoke one,' she said, 'and it made me vomit! I guess I am free at last!'

Tobacco is a drug. The origin of our word 'pharmacy' is a Greek word for 'the use or administering of drugs,' *pharmakeia*. However, *pharmakeia* also means 'sorcery and magic arts' and is 'often found in connection with idolatry and fostered by it' (Thayer). In other words, the Greeks linked the taking of drugs with the spiritual realm of the occult, the stamping ground of Satan and his minions. When a person submits to the rule of drugs, he or she allows these substances to occupy a key, often controlling, place in life, and the prerogative of God is usurped.

With any drug, such as tobacco, one can only guess how the soul crosses the boundary between *using the substance* and where the smoker becomes invaded by a demon who will then *abuse the person*. Though I have said that the addiction to tobacco may well remain at the physical level for many people (not a healthy situation anyway), the person with an evil spirit of 'Tobacco,' or some such, finds he has an extraordinary fight on his hands even to contemplate giving up the habit.

It was so in the case of Pauline. She was a slight woman who, with her husband, had become a Christian through a television ministry. When they joined a local church, they began to feel that they should give up smoking. They wanted to be good witnesses to their old friends. Mac, her husband, had little trouble shaking the habit, but Pauline suffered greatly and could not get free of it. She began to show signs of depression and an old sense of worthlessness began to afflict her.

She came for counselling for the problem, which was degenerating into self-loathing at a frightening speed. Her pastor and her husband had become worried she might do some harm to herself, a thought that had never come to her before she met Christ. This was a new, and quite uncharacteristic pattern.

'I don't know what has come over me,' Pauline said.

Well, I discovered her background had included some occult involvement. This, and some other factors, led toward deliverance. At the conclusion of the ministry, I said, 'In the Name of the Lord Jesus Christ, if there are any more demons in or around this woman, you will reveal yourselves, now!'

At once the woman's voice, with an extraordinary harshness, gasped, *'Tobacco!'* She renounced it, I commanded it, and she was instantly set free from the habit, and remained victorious for three years.

Then tragedy struck her young family. In the stress of it, she started to smoke again. This time the habit multiplied rapidly. Soon she was smoking six packs a day. Never a very robust person, Pauline began to lose weight, dark circles appeared under her eyes. Her physician said, 'Pauline, at the rate you are going, you will never die of cancer. You will die before it has a chance. You will die of smoke!'

During this period of her life, Pauline repented many times. She sought the laying-on-of hands, anointing, prayer on the church prayer chain, in fact everything she could imagine, but the habit actually increased. She asked to see me.

When she arrived at my office, I thought she might die before she could sit down! The coat I hung up in the closet, and everything about her, smelled of tobacco smoke. We tried everything we had done previously, but to no effect. Only now did I stop to pray specifically, 'Lord Jesus. You are the

Lord, our Healer and Deliverer. Please tell me what we must do to save this poor woman.'

The response came into my mind as if he was saying, 'Ask her what kind of cigarettes she smokes!' When I posed the question, Pauline dejectedly answered, 'Mentholated cigarettes . . .'

In a flash I felt I understood why we had been unsuccessful so far. She was not suffering from demons of tobacco, but of another substance, *menthol,* which is another drug, 'a secondary terpenoid alcohol.'

Pauline was delivered manifestly from a demon which had made her dangerously dependent on menthol. The sudden difference in her was absolutely spectacular. She leapt to her feet with a great shout of joy. Not only was she free from the smoking problem, but when she went to her physician next day, he could not believe the change he saw. She reported to me, 'He said it's is like I have new lungs!' And all this was within twenty-four hours of her deliverance! Does the Lord still do miracles? Ask Pauline! Ask her doctor!

The reader will not be surprised to learn that other drug addictions can sometimes be dealt with by deliverance. Dependencies of many kinds are not only signs of improper and degrading 'crutches,' they harm God's beloved children physically and mentally, emotionally and spiritually. No one still submitted to the governorship of drugs can enjoy the full liberty that belongs to a child of God.

~ 18 ~

Manifestations and Clues
Some 'Exotic' Happenings in Deliverance

The reader may wonder why I have not referred to some of the more sensational elements of deliverance ministry. I have refrained in order to keep focussed on the solid reality of how Jesus Christ mends his people's lives. However, now that I have established these principles, I will refer to some of the more 'exotic' possibilities one can encounter.

The personality of demons can be revealed through their words. These are spoken through the mouth of the demonized person. Sometimes they abuse the person's vocal chords so their voice sounds quite different. Often they will whine and wheedle, shout, curse, blaspheme and express all kinds of emotions including rage, hatred, fear, panic. They can sound sly and cunning, they will try to make deals to save themselves from their fate, they will lie, and deceive if they can. They can threaten awful things to the minister, who, because he or she is a person of prayer who does not trust in his own self, but in God, will treat them with fearlessness and contempt. He knows that the Lord Jesus is more than willing and able to keep him, and those he loves, totally safe.

When commanded in the name of the Lord Jesus Christ, demons can be forced to tell the truth, to speak in English, and can be brought out of hiding. Their nature is like their master, the devil's, so they will lie as often as they can get away with it. The Spirit-filled Christian will discern when they are lying and will often experience instantaneous knowledge of the truth that the demon is trying to conceal.

For several years, at the start of my work in deliverance, I used often to hear evil spirits speaking. I reflect that I was still discovering their ways and perhaps God needed to teach me through these manifestations.

I have said all I need, save to encourage readers to be certain that demons are not a fraction as clever as they make themselves out to be. Though they may boast and brag, and try to convince us that they are invincible, the gates of hell cannot prevail against the church (Matt 16:18). The discerning Christian, however, will not quickly dismiss all that a demon says. They often give themselves away by their words.

Once, we had a young professional woman living with us for three months, after she had lost her job because of her strange behaviour. She was juggling with five 'personalities.' She adopted each of them when appropriate for the different activities of her life. She was our first of several cases of so-called 'MPD' – multiple personality disorder.

Alice was quite unusual in my experience because I have found that lasting and complete deliverance can generally be accomplished at one sitting. I had spent many hours with her. Toward the end of her stay with us, I found Alice in our kitchen with a knife on her hand. She had a distant, tearful look. I asked her what she was thinking.

'I am going to harm myself,' she said.

'Oh no, you are not! Not in this house!' I told her. 'You have come too far for that!'

When she was sitting down, I felt a surging sense of

frustration which I recognized as a moving of the Holy Spirit. I demanded, in no uncertain terms, 'Spirit, you *cannot* hide any longer. I *command* you in the Name of Jesus Christ, *give* me your name.'

Alice shrank back. Her lips twisted, and malevolence was written all over her face. She ground her teeth, then spat out the word, '*Insanity!*' We immediately prayed accordingly, and she was delivered. As if the Lord was sealing her completed salvation, within a few days she received an offer of work. It turned out to be in a highly stressful area of her profession. She took the job, and did not look back.

Physical symptoms were often manifested by sufferers in my early years. People would be thrown back in their seat. This happened so frequently that I had to make sure they were in a high-backed chair. Sometimes, they would be jerked sideways. When a person moved quite violently, as they often did, I was afraid they would dislocate something. After one episode, a chiropractor who had sent a woman to see me, said, 'She hardly had a bone in its right place when I saw her next day.'

Rarely, people would fall to the floor and writhe, even foaming at the mouth. Those who had invited demonic indwelling through the practice of Satanism, prayer to the devil, or practice of some animistic religion, were the most demonstrative. Often, those who had entertained serious suicidal thoughts, or had made real attempts on their own lives, would suddenly grasp at their own throats. There, before my eyes, I would see someone actually throttling himself. I must admit that I often resorted to breaking their grip with my own hands. I recall once knowing that my hands were not going to win. The demon was killing the woman in my own living room! It was then I prayed with total energy, and the grip suddenly slackened. From then on, I dealt with all such demonstrations of the suicide spirit by prayer, and had no more trouble.

In 1973, the morning after a particularly 'active' deliverance session, I prayed like this: '*Dear Lord Jesus. I know that when you came down from the Mount of Transfiguration, a demon threw the boy, whom your disciples had been trying to heal, to the ground in a convulsion* (Mark 9:20). *If that happened in front of you, it may be that I have to see these demonstrations, too. But, if it is all right with you, I would love them to stop.*'

I have rarely seen another demonic demonstration from that day to this! Is it true in this ministry that we often do not have, because we do not ask?

~ 19 ~

Reflections

Deliverance Today and the Word of God:
Personal Preparation of the Minister and the Counsellee:
a Prayer of Exorcism

e have considered, now, the Scriptural authority for the Christ-initiated ministry of deliverance, and some of this healing work through church history. I have written from the perspective of a practical minister who takes the eternal character of God seriously. Of course, the validity of these experiences has to be submitted to the test of Holy Scripture. I have attempted to give Biblical data, as I have written. However, critical minds will always remain open to further questions about a Christian's testimony. I will now try to present some of the difficulties I have faced in dealing with my own issues with the ministry of deliverance.

First, I have had to ask myself if the experiences I have accumulated stand the scrutiny of Scripture, the absolute standard for spiritual truth. I ponder the question in the light of the Lord Jesus' profound statement, the night of his betrayal, concerning the work of the Holy Spirit: *'But when he, the Spirit of truth, comes, he will guide you into all truth. . . . He will bring glory to me by taking from what is mine and making it known to you'* (John 16:13-14). For two thousand years the Almighty has been revealing his grace in

160

ways that have often astounded his children. On the other hand, for just as long, people have also claimed revelation from 'on High' to back up all kinds of cranky ideas.

The essential issue is, do the happenings I have witnessed reflect the heart of God as he has revealed it in Scripture? I hope that the preceding chapters do redound to the glory of the Lord Jesus Christ.

The fact that the histories I have recorded may not always bear precise comparison in all points with accounts from God's word, does not undermine their validity, *if* they survive the acid-test of conformity to the revealed mind of God. Each reader must make his or her own assessment accordingly.

Consider, for example, Chapter 16. There I dealt with what is sometimes called 'generational sin.' In the early 1970s, long before I had read of such a phenomenon, I observed that particularly 'nasty' behaviour seemed to flow down from one generation to the next. I pondered this as I struggled with the enormous problems so many people endured in their characters or experiences, which reflected similar or identical flaws in a parent and, often, grandparent. I prayed for enlightenment.

The minister of deliverance needs to desire the highest personal integrity and purest truth. Every counselling session should always be covered by deep prayer and an awareness that it was the Holy Name of Jesus and the power of his Precious Blood that enables the work of healing to be accomplished. Often I would pray with silent urgency, deep in my spirit, when, in the midst of listening to people's life-stories, I became utterly perplexed. Many were the occasions when I could not see a direct application of a specific word from the Bible, and nothing that I knew from psychology, or past experience, helped. Sometimes the Holy Spirit would supply to my mind a precise verse, or partial verse, which fitted the situation perfectly. Another time he would put a fragment of certain knowledge into my mind. Then I just *knew* what the answer was, and so, by the results of blessing and new life, it proved to be.

One day, in my private devotions, I was meditating on the Ten Commandments. It was then that God's warning in the second commandment seemed to fit so many circumstances. God was *'punishing the children for the sin of the fathers to the third and fourth generation of those who hate [him]'* (Exod. 20:5).

I felt an argument arising in my heart, based on the word of God where he says, *'In those days people will no longer say, "The fathers have eaten sour grapes, and the children's teeth are set on edge." Instead, everyone will die for his own sin; whoever eats sour grapes – his own teeth will be set on edge'* (Jer. 31:29-30).

When I saw that the prophet's words were an introduction to the coming days of the New Covenant, I pondered furiously before the Lord. So many lives showed that very often indeed children were still being seriously hurt by parents' sin, repeating their sin one generation after another. And here we were, living two thousand years after the redeeming work of Christ had been completed. What could explain this apparent inheritance of evil? Why were the 'sour grapes' eaten by the fathers still setting the children's teeth on edge?

Then I began to understand that Jeremiah was referring to those people who would *'know the Lord'* (Jer. 31:34). In other words, children of *believers* would not suffer their teeth being 'set on edge' because of the sins of their parents or forefathers!

The people I was dealing with were usually *first generation* believers. Their parents were not Christians, but unbelievers. Therefore, they were acting like pre-New Covenant people, and so could still suffer under the terms of the Law, including the second Commandment. Yes. It appeared as if God, our unchanging God, was still *visiting the iniquity of the fathers upon the children unto the third and fourth generation of them that hate [him]'* (Exod. 20:5 KJV).

The next issue was, even if this is so, could I be sure that demons were involved in the sinful 'inheritance'? In dealing with spiritual problems the minister is always dealing with the invisible. The existence of spiritual problems is evidenced by the serious experiences of the individual. One cannot measure, weigh or see the cause of the problem, whether demonically instigated or not. We can only observe the results it is having in the person's life.

This was the case when Jesus crossed over the Sea of Galilee and encountered the man with demons. Their brutalizing effects are graphically described in Mark 5. In answer to the Lord's question, *'What is your name?'* the evil spirit answered *'My name is Legion, for we are many'* (Mark 5:9). Here, the Lord felt it necessary to make the enquiry, perhaps to make a teaching point for the Disciples' benefit. However, it appears the spirit answered truthfully for the response was accepted by Christ.

I determined, in early years, that I would count myself as a disciple who could learn from Christ's handling of that particular situation. So, because of confidence given me in the power of prayer to force evil spirits to obey any command given them in the Name of the Lord Jesus Christ, I sometimes spoke to them.

I commanded them to give their names, and they did. Sometimes they hedged, and quibbled, but they could not resist for long. Once they had given their names I might demand to know when they had gained access to the individual. Many times the response came identifying an event or moment in the individual's life.

Do we need the exact names of demons? I do not think this is always critical to success. Appendix III provides a list of some I have come across grouped together in 'families' for convenience. Some are very common. But once, a smartly dressed professional woman appeared on my doorstep, unexpectedly. I was quite unprepared, and even more surprised when, while she was still standing in the entrance hall, I 'saw' the appearance of a fiery dragon in her midriff. I called in my heart to God, 'Lord Jesus! What is *that?*' Immediately the clear word '*Craven*' came to my mind.

When the lady was seated, I told her what I had seen, calling it by a name I had dealt with before: '*Cowardice.*' Because the woman understood these things, and was up to date with her confession, she renounced that spirit and, in the Name of the Lord Jesus Christ, I bound it, and commanded it to go. To my astonishment, I could still 'see' the 'dragon.' The woman sat quietly. In a flash, I repeated my words of command, but used the name '*Craven spirit.*' The woman instantly gasped, doubled up, and sat back with a glorious, 'Thank you Jesus!' and tears in her eyes.

Sometimes, especially when I was having difficulty with understanding exactly what the sufferer was experiencing, the demon would identify an ancestor of the person, and even the event in that forebear's life when the spirit had first 'locked-on' to the family-line. The satisfaction that this was true came when we dealt with the problem as the demon described it, and the present generation person was manifestly set free, immediately. This was glorious!

Another area of speculation concerns the question, where should we send infesting demons? I know of highly esteemed ministers who command evil spirits to go ' into the abyss,' or 'into the deepest sea.' In the case of the Gadarene demoniac, the infested pigs ran down the slope and were drowned *'in the sea.'* Certainly, the Jews looked upon the ocean as a fearful place, where dwelt the monster, the *'great Leviathan.'* And did not Jesus think that drowning *'in the depths of the sea'* would be a fitting end for anyone who causes one of his believing *'little ones'* to sin? (Matt. 18:6).

In this connection, I was influenced by the work of the Bishop of Exeter's Commission on Exorcism.[1] Robert Mortimer's impressive trans-denominational team suggested prayers before, during and after an exorcism. A prayer for exorcism includes these words: *'I command you, every evil spirit, in the Name of God the Father Almighty, in the Name of Jesus Christ his only Son, and in the name of the Holy Spirit, that harming no one you depart from this creature of God, N., and return to the place appointed you, there to remain forever'* (p. 37). Another prayer speaks of *'the place appointed them'* (p. 44).

The need for confession of personal sin would be difficult to exaggerate. Hard though it may be to believe, often I have come across new Christians who were never taught that repentance means not only turning *to* Christ, but *away from* sin. Surprisingly, the need to renounce the devil and all his works, the evil desires of the flesh and of the world, is often not taught to new believers.

My general practice is, first, to make certain the person makes a full confession of faith and of sins, as may be necessary to be as near pure before God as possible. They renounce *'the devil and all his works, the evil desires of the flesh and of the world'* any spirits that have been recognized, and any others that might be oppressing them. Then, I name the spirits also, plus any that spring into mind, saying next something like this, addressing the evil spirits: *'This man/woman/boy/girl is a child of God, washed in the Blood of the Lamb, and you have no right to afflict him/her. I bind you all, in the name of the Lord Jesus Christ, and command you to leave this person now, and go to the place prepared for you!'*

Why do I not use the name of the Trinity? I have found that the power of the Christian ministering deliverance lies predominantly in the fact that he or she represents the person of the Lord Jesus Christ. His is the name at which demons tremble and to which they submit. It is the name of *'the LORD Jesus Christ'* which is so powerful, not simply the name of 'Jesus.' I have come across deceiving 'Jesus' spirits, false christs, which are effective in their ability to delude people. Some demonized people who could speak the name of *'Jesus'* found it physically impossible to say, *'Lord Jesus Christ.'* **It is always the lordship of Jesus Christ that is at stake in the believer's life,** and demons will resist leaving as long as they can, until they feel the full weight of the Christian's faith in the LORD.

Among other questions that have arisen for me as I have attempted to discover the will of God in this work, is this: how can I be sure that deliverance prayers were always vital for a Christian person to be set free from their dread, murderous anger, oppression, vile habits, immorality, or other problem? Were not many such problems fully dealt with by God's grace through the cleansing of the psyche that comes with complete honesty, confession, and the assurance of forgiveness that is authenticated by the word of God?

Making a full confession, often for the first time in their life, will bring a person tremendous relief. Sometimes this has been so great, so 'tangible,' that I have thought that this was all that was needed to help the person, they seemed so blessed. But then, often deliverance has manifestly occurred at the next stage, with renunciation, binding and authoritative command in Jesus' name. Experience has shown that the additional prayers of deliverance often were essential.

Sometimes, with the words of delivering authority, joyful people have felt 'something' leave their body. Others have been thrilled by a sudden lifting of weight from their back or head. Others might sense a sudden relief of pressure from an area of the head or body. Sometimes a person's sight is brightened so they physically see more clearly. I have known a few people to see certain colours for the first time. Other physical manifestations can happen, but the experience, whatever it may be, is conclusive for the individual. The feeling of internal light flooding one is common. 'Oh!' said one lady, 'I feel like an apple that has been cored!'

There are many questions that sensitive Christians will always wisely ask about deliverance ministry, especially because there have been incidents where well-meaning would-be 'deliverers' have said and done some unloving or unwise things. But I fear the same foolishness can also be seen in every other aspect of ministry.

The ministry which brings the kind of liberty of which I have written is not easy to measure objectively. In a culture trained in the scientific method we like to be able to 'prove' things. In deliverance work, as with all exercises of faith, the proof lies in the experience of those who have put it to the test. It may not be satisfactorily explicable to some Christians, but for those who have enjoyed the benefits, and who delight to give the glory to God, some questions may be merely academic. Happily, the blessings give many cause to reflect upon similarities with happenings in the New Testament and Early church.

Note

1. Mortimer, Robert, *Exorcism – The Findings of a Commission commissioned by the Bishop of Exeter*, Dom Robert Petitpierre, ed. (London: SPCK, 1972).

~ 20 ~

Afterword

The Almighty and unchanging Father of lights, the God and Father of our Lord Jesus Christ, has created a world which no man can comprehend. The mysteries of good and evil, however, have been revealed in the person of Jesus of Nazareth. He faced the puzzling questions of life with a pure and peaceable wisdom. Our Lord recognized, with boundless inner certainty, the present reality of the spirit-world. He knew the immediacy of his Father's Spirit and of the holy angels.

Jesus was so indwelt by the Spirit that he could disclaim his words as his own, but said they emanated from his Father in heaven. When Jesus taught, encouraged or rebuked, it was God who spoke. Christ's compassion was that of the Creator himself. When Jesus healed and delivered, it was God who ministered to the suffering people. The Son of God is *'the same yesterday and today and forever'* (Heb. 13:8). We are fond of saying this, but familiarity can sometimes strike a hollow note.

Yes. Jesus still teaches, encourages and, when necessary, rebukes the children he loves. Many years ago, he rebuked me for my unbelief in the Biblical description of the spirit-world. He taught me to trust his written word in every detail, and then went on to prove in the lives of over two thousand souls the delivering grace that is encompassed within his total redeeming love.

How hard it is for the flesh to grasp what is not visible, to receive what flies in the face of the post-modern mind-set. But there again, it was hard for the Jews of Christ's day, too. Humanity is characterized by sinful, obtuse arrogance. We have a reluctance to believe the good and the perfect, but a readiness to embrace the corrupt and manipulable. This means that men and women tend, remorselessly, to reject what they cannot control. We want our own way.

Our present day is marked by society's increasing rebellion against any authority whatsoever. In the realm of the supernatural, rejecting the divine authority of Almighty God we fall before the hidden and counterfeit agenda of Satan. Which is why we may see more evidence of demonization in the third millennium.

The truth is, *'It is a dreadful thing to fall into the hands of the living God'* (Heb. 10:31). Because we are weak, and our faith is so often merely mental, we steer clear of the risk of actually *experiencing* what it is like to trust ourselves into his hands. To have to *rely* on him, in whom we say we believe, in a critically threatening situation, means we have to exercise extraordinary faith – the Christian kind. Such faith recognizes that every spiritually dangerous circumstance truly bears within it an immense promise. We forget the Cross to our peril.

Christians, I fear, are as prone as any to keep God at a distance. We, too, are befouled by the sticky fingers of the arch-rebel. We hesitate to yield to God's absolute authority. We like to keep God where he can be understood, satisfying our personal theology, within the reach of our limited minds, in other words, under our mental control.

But God will not work to the extent of his complete will under these restrictions. He requires faith from us, ideally the kind that goes as far as Christ's faith went. Because he requires faith, he is ready to empower us with it. Are we not, however, more likely to try to work things out for ourselves than to *ask him* for additional faith?

To venture into the realm of spiritual warfare, in the sense of undertaking the deliverance of human beings from the thrall of Satan, requires risk-taking. It requires an understanding of God's will as revealed to us in his written word, and by the person who *is 'the Word.'* Once one decides to take the risk of obeying God in any sphere of activity, including deliverance ministry, one can trust God to continue teaching and encouraging. We rely on his enablement.

If I have conveyed anything, I hope it might be something of the joy that Christ wants to give to the Christian who will take his instruction seriously. *'He called his twelve disciples to him and gave them authority to drive out evil spirits'* (Matt. 10:1). It is no use arguing, 'I am not one of the Twelve! *I am just me!'* His orders to us are identical to those he gave to his first followers. On the night before his Crucifixion, at the last supper, Jesus prayed for his disciples: *'My prayer is not for them alone. I pray also for those who will believe in me through their message, that all of them may be one, Father, just as you are in me and I am in you'* (John 17:20-21a).

Listen to Jesus' final command to the Twelve, before his Ascension: *'All authority in heaven and on earth has been given to me. Therefore go and make disciples of all nations, baptizing them in the name of the Father and of the Son and of the Holy Spirit, and teaching them to obey everything I have commanded you'* (Matt. 28:18-20).

The power of the Cross is all-sufficient for human beings

to have Christ's gift of the fullness of life (John 10:10). Yet, for some, the ongoing process of sanctification, or 'living in the Spirit,' is radically enhanced after deliverance. I have outlined the steps that can be undertaken. The appendices at the end of the book give some useful summaries.

To stand before Christ on 'that great day,' only to discover that we had within our grasp 'talents' for deliverance which we never invested for the glory of God, would be devastating. For the help of countless demonically afflicted souls, I pray Christians will be strong and of good courage. Jesus, our Lord, shares with his people his victory, nothing less than the overcoming of the world, the flesh and the devil.

Let none be deaf to his gracious and often repeated words, *'Do not be afraid.'* They are Christ's personal exhortation to all who have ears to hear.

To see people brought to complete liberty, who had been imprisoned as securely by demons as any inmate jailed inside a penitentiary, is to see God's glory. To witness them go on with fulfilled, balanced lives, sometimes becoming leaders or counsellors in the wonderful work of the Gospel, is one of the greatest possible privileges.

I have written as one who was the least inclined toward and totally unequipped for this work when first I heard my friend, Edgar Trout, in Plymouth, long ago. What I witnessed of the Lord Jesus in and through him exposed in me a great hunger to be filled with the Holy Spirit for Christ's service. From then on, as I have tried to show, it was learning to be obedient, and to be willing to try to follow wherever our Lord and Master led. No doubt I made many mistakes, but none would have been as grievous as failing to let my heart be set on fire for his suffering people.

I pray some who read these lines will seek from the Lord

his confirmation to adopt deliverance as an element in their practical love for God and for their neighbours. The way of the pilgrim is very exciting, very blessed! Hallelujah!

Glossary

Deliverance
'Deliverance' means 'the act of expelling evil spirits or demons by adjuration in the Name of Jesus Christ and through his power' (Burgess 1988, 290).[1] In the first act of deliverance ministry recorded in Mark, Jesus commands the unclean spirit, *'come out of him'* (Mark 1:25). The term 'exorcism' as a synonym of 'deliverance' is found historically in Christianity up to modern times (Cross 1958, 485). The subject of exorcism focuses on demons: one exorcises demons, not people. People are the subject of deliverance; they receive deliverance from demons. Neither 'exorcist' nor 'exorcism' appear in the Bible to describe the casting out of spirits by Christ or any of his disciples.

In Biblical terms, deliverance was also given to those who were 'cured of evil spirits' (Luke 8:2), Dickason says (1987, 269-70). Luke 6:18 records, *'Those troubled [vexed, tormented, harassed] (ἐνοχλούμενοι – ĕnŏchloumenoi) by evil spirits were cured.'* In both of these instances the Greek verb θεραπεύω (therapeuō), which may be translated to 'cure,' 'heal,' 'restore to health' (Thayer 1977, 288), is used.

Synonymous language for deliverance includes breaking of spiritual bondage (Anderson 1990) and liberation of people involving 'freedom for service of God and man' (Neil-Smith 1974, 31), as well as the expelling of evil forces, or demons.

---

1. For references in this section see Selected Biography, p. 195.

Deliverance does not, however, do away with temptation which is a recurring phenomenon for all humankind (ibid., 32), as it was for Christ (Heb. 4:15).

Deliverance ministry includes counselling, discerning of spirits and understanding Satanic influence. Deliverance ministry deals with the breaking of spiritual bondage and culminates in the individual's freedom from the evil spirit(s). The term 'deliverance' occurs often to describe the whole scope of this ministry (Dickason 1987; Unger 1991; Warner 1991; White 1990; and others).

Demons and Evil Spirits

The terms 'demons' and 'evil spirits' describe 'divinely created supernatural beings' who, with their leader Satan, rebelled against God (Elwell 1988, 610). Demons have always been thought by many to be 'fallen angels' (ibid., Dickason 1987, 24). Satan uses demons as emissaries for promoting his design to thwart God's plans (Ryrie 1981, 164). They may have personal names and be identified with such particular roles or functions as lying, murder, suicide, lust, depression or fear (Elwell 1988, 610). Demons 'tempt, deceive and delude people so as to bring them to eternal damnation.' They also oppose God by attacking, oppressing, hindering and accusing the people of God (ibid. 611).

Demonization

'Demonized' is from the Bible's verb δαιμονίζομαι (daimon-izomai), 'to be under the power of a demon' (Thayer 1977, 123). It is a term preferred by many writers to describe demonic presence in human life (Kraft 1992, 35-7; Murphy 1990, 57; Dickason 1987, 37; Unger 1991). This term, with its cognates, is used to describe those over whom Satan, 'through his evil spirits, exercises direct, partial control over one or more areas of the life of a human being' (Murphy 1990, 57).

'Demonization' is a noun derived from 'demonized.' In Pennoyer's view, 'demonization is a personal relationship; the imposition of an evil spirit into the life of a human being' (Wagner and Pennoyer 1990, 250). The present author agrees, while adding that 'demonization' occurs whenever an evil spirit has a domineering role regardless of its location – whether within or without a person. Location, therefore, is not of the essence of demonization. Kraft, however, defines 'demonization' as the New Testament term which refers to any degree of demonic activity from inside a person (1990, 276). Dickason agrees, saying it is 'demon caused passivity or control due to a demon's residing within a person' (1987, 40).

Demonic Obsession
Some authorities have described three states of demonization: 'oppression,' 'obsession' and 'possession' (Burgess 1988, 292). These are seen as progressive in severity (ibid.). But I agree with Dickason (1987, 40) and Green (1981), disagree. Green says in his discussion of δαιμονίζομαι (daimonizomai): 'The modern distinction between oppression and possession has no basis in the Greek New Testament' (131). In other words, the Bible does not make Burgess' kind of distinction. Unger says 'all demonic invasion is demonization whatever [the] degree of mildness or severity' (1991, 98).

The word 'obsession' is not connected with the demonic in Scripture. According to Bubeck (1975), obsession 'traditionally has meant the subject's uncontrollable preoccupation with demonic forces or phenomena' (83). Such obsession requires deliverance steps.

Demon-possession

'Demon-possession,' 'demon possessed' and 'devil possessed' were expressions popularized through the King James Version of the Bible, says Murphy (1992, 49). He, and the authorities already quoted, prefer to use 'demonization.' Yet 'demon possession' is a term used by some for the state of an individual into whose body the evil spirit(s) or demon(s) or other entities have entered to take control (Sargant 1973, 44; Ryrie 1981, 165; Burnett 1988). Believers and unbelievers alike are affected and influenced by demonic activity, 'but not all are possessed' (Ryrie 1981, 165).

Discernment

Discernment is another way of expressing to 'look beneath the surface' to 'distinguish between spirits' (1 Cor. 12:10). Discernment is 'the ability to know the spirits that are from God and those that are evil' (Southard 1986, 133). This gift of the Spirit is popularly called 'spiritual discernment,' or 'discerning of spirits' (1 Cor. 12:10 KJV).

Steps to Deliverance

1. The Gospel of Christ is a full and whole Gospel. It embraces:
   a. Repentance, Salvation, Sanctification, Healing, Deliverance and Teaching.

2. Repentance, involving a wholehearted commitment to Jesus Christ and an intention to live a godly lifestyle, is a vital matter in deliverance (Matt. 12:43-45). Repentance:
   a. removes the devil's 'footholds' (Eph. 4:27) from a person's life.
   b. prevents a return of the demon (Matt. 12:43-45).
   c. is closely linked to healing (Luke 5:23-24 – paralysed man; James 5:16 – confess your sins).

3. Nine steps to deliverance:
   a. Humble yourself.
   b. Be absolutely honest.
   c. Confess and repent for all sins of the flesh.
   d. Repent and renounce all occult involvement and idolatry.
   e. Confess and renounce all ancestral involvement in the occult and idolatry.
   f. Forgive all who have sinned against you.

g. Call on the Name of the Lord.

h. Renounce and bind evil spirits and command them to leave.

i. Destroy all charms, amulets, talismans, books, records, tapes or souvenirs which have idolatrous or occult meaning. (Beware of some 'rock' music.)

4. Repentance should cover the Ten Commandments (Exod. 20), and the Seven Deadly Sins: pride, anger, lust, envy, gluttony, avarice (love of money) and sloth (laziness). Ministers should give assurance of God's forgiveness to those who truly repent (John 20:23).

5. A form of deliverance command: *'In the Name of the Lord Jesus Christ, and by the power of his Precious Blood, I bind every spirit of . . . and command you to leave me (or . . . this child of God), and go to the place prepared for you, harming nobody, now. AMEN.'*

6. Nine reasons why full deliverance may be missed:
   a. Lack of true repentance/renunciation.
   b. Failure to confess certain sins.
   c. Self-deception about reasons for obtaining deliverance.
   d. Failure to forgive others – and self (after confession).
   e. Failure to break with the occult.
   f. Affection for old sin and those associated with it (justifying a mindset which says 'my sins led me to Christ').
   g. Double-mindedness or equivocation about truly serving Christ.
   h. Voluntary return to old sins.

  i. Listening to a deceiving spirit, even being sorry for it!

7. Nine main requirements for keeping deliverance:
   a. Christ must be Saviour *and* Lord over every area of life.
   b. Every day, ask God to fill you with his Holy Spirit (Eph. 5:18).
   c. Live by the Word of God (John 8:31-32).
   d. Meditate on the word of God (Psalm 119; 2 Tim. 3:16-17).
   e. Keep on the whole armour of God (Eph. 6:10-18).
   f. Become a person who has a devout frame of mind all day long, *praying always* (1 Thess. 5:16).
   g. Have a thankful, rejoicing purpose, always being ready to bear witness to your Saviour, Jesus (Phil. 4:4-7; 1 Peter 3:15).
   h. Cultivate right friends and relationships.
   i. Be faithful in church participation, helping and supporting its ministry and outreach.

Profiles of Demonic Attack

Like a city whose walls are broken down is a man who lacks self-control (Prov. 25:28).

1. Satan attacks a person, looking for weaknesses in his/her defence.
   A. Demons work to destroy every aspect of human peace:
      i. Inner personal harmony.
      ii. Peace of mind.
      iii. Physical well-being.
      iv. Harmonious relationships – especially with those closest to us.
      v. Harmonious adjustment to external circumstances.

   B. Great distinctive mark of demon activity is *restlessness*.

   C. They operate either from outside the body or from inside:
      i. If they are outside, we must resist them:
         a. James 4:7 – *Submit yourselves, then, to God. Resist the devil, and he will flee from you.*
         b. 1 Peter 5:8-9 – *Be self-controlled and alert. Your enemy the devil prowls around like a*

roaring lion looking for someone to devour. Resist him, standing firm in the faith.

ii. If they are on the inside, following Christ's example, we must expel them:

    a. Matt. 8:16-17 – *When evening came, many who were demon-possessed were brought to him, and he drove out the spirits with a word and healed all the sick. This was to fulfil what was spoken through the prophet Isaiah: 'He took up our infirmities and carried our diseases.'*

    b. Mark 1:39 – *So [Jesus] travelled throughout Galilee, preaching in their synagogues and driving out demons.*

    c. Mark 16:17 – *And these signs will accompany those who believe: In my name they will drive out demons.*

2. How spirits can be 'picked up.'

    A. Habitual or violent breaking of any of the Ten Commandments (Exodus 20), or any of the other commands of God, e.g. Lev. 18 and 19.

      i. 2nd Commandment – includes occult (Deut. 18:9-13).

      ii. 3rd Commandment – includes oaths of a secret nature.

      iii. 6th Commandment – includes abortion and suicide.

      iv. 7th Commandment – includes fornication, rape, homosexuality, incest, molesting.

      v. Failure to love – God, neighbour, self.

B. Lifestyle under any of the 'Seven Deadly Sins':
   i. Pride, Anger, Lust, Envy, Gluttony, Avarice, Sloth.
      a. Gluttony includes drunkenness, drug abuse.
      b. Avarice may include failure to tithe.

C. Inheritance:
   i. Ancestral occult background (witchcraft, mediumship, divination, etc.).
   ii. Curses, upon self or ancestors.
   iii. Any strong element in the family line that broke anything in A and B, above, e.g. violence, whoredom.

D. Occult involvement:
   i. Personally taking part.
   ii. Being present when others were dabbling.

E. Sexual immorality:
   i. Promiscuity, homosexuality, adultery, lust, pornography, etc. (see A).

F. Accident, or trauma.

G. Involvement with demonic people, demonic places or things:
   i. Fetishes, souvenirs, etc., visits to temples and shrines of non-Christian religions.

H. Curses: See Deut. 28 for the Curses.

I. Hypnotism, Passivity.

J. False religions:
i. Non-Christian religions.
   a. *I [Jesus Christ] am the [narrow] gate, the way, the truth and the life* (John 10:7,9).
   b. *No one comes to the Father except through me [Jesus Christ]* (John 14:6).
   c. *For through [Jesus Christ] we ... have access to the Father by One Spirit* (Eph. 2:18).
ii. The New Age Movement:
   a. To seek spiritual help from other than the One True God is to worship that 'helper' spirit-guide, whatever name it goes under.
   b. The NAM may bring demonic afflictions upon one's future generations (Exod. 20:4-6). *(Beware all occult, psychic involvement.)*
   c. Other gods are demons (Lev. 17:7; Deut. 32:17; 2 Chron. 11:15; Ps. 106:37; 1 Cor. 10:20).
   d. Humankind is forbidden to contact other spirits (Deut.13:1-5; 18:9-14).
iii. Heresies/Cults:
   a. Departures from *the faith that was once for all entrusted to the saints* (Jude 3).
   b. *Deceiving spirits and things taught by demons draw unbelievers into error [fads, excesses]* (1 Tim. 4:1-2).
   c. *False teachers ... secretly introduce destructive heresies* e.g. Jehovah's Witnesses, Mormons, Theosophy, Christian Science, etc. (2 Peter 2:1-2).
   d. The antichrist spirit is in the world, in human beings, including, possibly, people from the church (1 John 2:18-23).

iv. Fantasy:
   a. May prove dangerous. It can open the mind to evil imagination, e.g. by playing '*Dungeons and Dragons.*'
v. Domination:
   a. Witchcraft and Satanic practices.
      (1) There are no 'good' demons. There is no such thing as 'good' magic.
      (2) 'White' and 'black' witchcraft and magic are all abhorrent to God and lead to hell. Natural 'magic' which is mere sleight of hand illusion, is not meant here.
      (3) Domination of one person by another is directly related to witchcraft, even though the dominator may not know it.

3. How evil spirits work:
   A. They attack the threefold nature of human beings:
      i. Body, spirit and soul:
         a. *And the Lord God formed man from the dust of the ground and breathed into his nostrils the breath of life, and man became a living being [soul]* (Gen. 2:7).
         b. *May your spirit, soul and body be kept blameless at the coming of our Lord Jesus Christ* (1 Thess. 5:23).
         c. Salvation is a *spirit* rebirth:
            (1) *I tell you the truth, unless a man is born of water and the Spirit, he cannot enter the kingdom of God* (John 3:5).
            (2) Contrast 'flesh' with 'spirit.' *Flesh gives birth to flesh, but the Spirit gives birth to spirit* (John 3:6).

186

(a) In Christ's and Paul's teaching, 'flesh' includes body and soul; 'spirit' is spirit: *The spirit is willing, but the flesh is weak* (Matt. 26:41; Romans, passim).

(3) When the spirit is reborn, the flesh is *affected*, the soul *changed*, but not yet heavenly perfect.

(a) The believer is *predestined to be conformed to the likeness of [Christ]* (Rom. 8:29).

(b) The command is: *Continue to work out your salvation with fear and trembling, for it is God who works in you to will and to act according to his good purpose* (Phil. 2:12,13).

(c) Spiritual people have *'the mind of Christ'* (understanding, reason, higher faculties of the soul).

d. The tripartite human nature is a spiritual instrument to communicate with God, who is Spirit.

(1) The conversation between the serpent and Eve in the Garden of Eden, announced that humankind is open to communication with evil spiritual forces.

(2) We pick up 'signals' from evil spirits.

(3) John Wesley says, 'The devil can more easily put a thought into a man's mind than we can whisper in his ear.'

4. Discerning of spirits.

A. Know your enemy! Do not be ignorant!

   i. Demons are 'persons without bodies,' sent to afflict humanity. They have feelings, intelligence, can hear and speak.

   ii. Their target is the human mind, to gain mental strongholds.

   iii. They attack the flesh (body and soul).

   iv. Demons hope to keep the human spirit in bondage, so sharing their fate, to spite God's saving purpose.

   v. Two words always betray illegal satanic influence: 'domination' and 'manipulation.'

   vi. Human, sin nature cannot discern between spirits unless one *hungers and thirsts for righteousness.*

     a. When reborn of the Spirit a person can learn to discern between the good and the evil spirit.

     b. *The ability to distinguish between spirits* is a gift of the Holy Spirit (1 Cor. 12:10).

     c. While not every person may have this gift, yet *every Christian*, through the indwelling Spirit of Jesus, *should learn* to recognize whether people are of God's Spirit or of the world's spirit (2 Cor. 5:16; 1 John 3:10).

     d. Are the spirits we are in touch with from God, or from Satan? *Dear friends, do not believe every spirit, but test the spirits to see whether they are from God, because many false prophets have gone out into the world. This is how you recognize the Spirit of God: Every spirit that acknowledges that Jesus Christ has come in the flesh is from God, but every spirit that does not acknowledge Jesus is not from God. This is the spirit of the antichrist, ...* (1 John 4:1-3).

e. Believers trust the Scriptures for their standard of spiritual judgment. *For the Word of God is living and active. Sharper than any double-edged sword, it penetrates even to the dividing of soul and spirit, joints and marrow; it judges the thoughts and attitudes of the heart* (Heb. 4:12).

f. Satan does not often appear in his false glory – he is a sly deceiver, a liar.

  (1) Jesus described him as a thief: *The thief comes only to steal and kill and destroy: I have come that they may have life, and have it to the full* (John 10:10).

  (2) People know that this Scripture describes their own experience with the devil:

  (3) A person with unnatural fear *feels* robbed of peace, company, sleep, generosity, etc.

  (4) Sometimes, a person just *knows*, with an uncanny sense, that evil is present in a situation.

5. Areas of Self-Defence.

  A. The three areas of self-defence to maintain are: *spiritual; moral; and physical.*

  i. Demon activity comes mainly in six forms which can affect any, or all three, of the above areas.

  a. Harassment

  b. Torment

c. Enticement
d. Driving or compelling
e. Enslavement
f. Defilement

B. Six realms where this activity (demonization) can be found:
[Note carefully: The presence of the following flaws in a person's life does not always mean demonization! In cases where demons have invaded a person's life there is an uncontrollable element, a sense of inescapable bondage to the problem. Confession, and decision to change, do not necessarily loosen a relentless 'grip.']
  i. Emotions:
     a. For example – fear, resentment, hatred, bitterness, rejection, terror, panic, self-hatred, violence.
  ii. Thoughts:
     a. The realm of the intellect. e.g., rebellion against God, pride, doubt, unbelief, indecision, confusion, perfectionism, procrastination, compromise, cowardice, fantasy, perverse humour, manipulation (of others), voices in the head, nightmares.
  iii. Sex:
     a. Such as – perversion, lust, pornography, adultery, whoredom, lesbianism, homo-sexuality, fornication, masturbation, fear of married sexuality.
  iv. Addictions:
     a. For example – drugs (prescribed sometimes,

as well as illicit), alcohol, gluttony, TV, tobacco, pornography, gambling.

v. The tongue:

   a. Such as – gossip, slander, lying, back-biting, faction, division, deception, unclean talk, filthy jokes, levity, blasphemy.

vi. The body:

   a. Including – undiagnosable sickness or pain, pain which moves around the body, and *possibly*: headaches (especially migraine), cramp, arthritis, allergies, tumours, seizures, giddiness.

Demonic 'Families'[1] Outline

MURDER
Murder
Hatred
Violence
Anger
Rage
Bitterness
Resentment
Temper
Abortion
Rebellion
Rejection
Cruelty
Torture
Spite
Stubbornness
Impatience
Self-righteous
Pride
Conceit
Vanity
Intolerance
Aggression

Belligerence
Criticism
Complaining
Unforgiveness

OCCULT
All 'dabbling'
Divination
Fortune-telling
Python
Ouija-board
Clairvoyance
Familiar
Medium
Channelling
Spirit-guide
Witchcraft
Water-witching
Sorcery
Tarot
Card-reading
Palm-reading
Crystals

Pendulums
Astral-travel
Hypnotism
Levitation
Numerology
Curiosity
Ghosts
Weird experiences

SUICIDE
Suicide
Self-pity
Selfishness
Self-centred
Self-rejection
Self-hatred
Shame
False guilt
Insecurity
Despair
Timidity
Shyness
Self-destruction

1. From an original idea of the Rev. Doug Warren.

Depression
Heaviness

RELIGIOUS
Cults
Non-Christian
  religions
Yoga
TM
New Age
Christian
  denominations
  (idolatrous,
  consuming
  loyalty to)
Superstition
Idolatry
Satanism
All religious
  excess
Secret societies

IMMORAL
Lust
Adultery
Fornication
Homosexual
Lesbian
Bestiality
Perversion
Pornography

Masturbation
Lasciviousness
Licentiousness
Prostitution
Whoredom
Rape
Brutality
Incest
Molestation
Divorce
Carousing
Concupiscence
Nymphomania
Satyr
Covetousness
Jealousy
Envy
Squandering
Avarice
Meanness
Foolishness
Stupidity
Sentimentality
Hypocrisy
Cheating
Deceiving
Stealing
Procrastination
Perfectionism
Rock
Sloth
Laziness

Drunkenness
Workaholism

**BODY
  AFFLICTION**
Acupuncture &
  acupressure
Drugs, licit &
  illicit
Alcohol
Tobacco
Nicotine
Tension
Stress
Allergies
Blindness
Deafness
Weakness
Impotence
Frigidity
Illnesses
Nervousness
Tattoo
Itch
Migraine

SPEECH
Blasphemy
Cursing
Swearing
Evil-speaking
Lying

False-witness
Levity
Boasting

DOUBT[1] **and
UNBELIEF**
Confusion

**FAMILY BACK-
GROUND**
Evil Inheritance

**CURSES
RECEIVED**

FEAR OF:
Death
Future
The unknown
Poverty
Specific persons
Loneliness
Betrayal

Rejection
The dark
Failure
- and other
phobias,
including fears
originating in
*films or
television* seen,
or other life-
experiences.

---

1. 'Doubt' and 'Unbelief' are *always* to be expected in a demonized person. They are best left to the end in deliverance session.

Selected Bibliography

Anderson, Neil T., *The Bondage Breaker* (Eugene: Harvest House, 1990). [Best seller; only writer with a militant attitude against demons who does not believe in exorcism, but relies on 'truth encounter' and self deliverance.]

—— *Released from Bondage* (San Bernardino: Here's Life, 1991). [True stories of people helped.]

—— *Walking Through the Darkness: Discerning God's Guidance in the New Age* (San Bernardino: Here's Life, 1991).

—— and Charles Mylander, *Setting Your Church Free* (Ventura, CA: Regal Books, 1994). [Spiritual warfare applied to a congregation.]

Bubeck, Mark I., *The Adversary – The Christian Versus Demon Activity* (Chicago: Moody, 1975). [Broke a lot of ground with this early focus.]

—— *Overcoming the Adversary – Warfare Praying Against Demon Activity* (Chicago: Moody, 1984).

—— *The Satanic Revival* (San Bernardino: Here's Life, 1991).

Burgess, Stanley M. and Gary B. McGee, eds., *Dictionary of Charismatic and Pentecostal Movements* (Grand Rapids: Zondervan, 1988).

Burnett, David, *Unearthly Powers – A Christian Perspective on Primal and Folk Religion* (Eastbourne, England: MARC [Monarch Publications], 1988).

Cross, F. L., ed., *Oxford Dictionary of the Christian Church* (London, Oxford University Press, 1958).

Dickason, C. Fred., *Demon Possession & the Christian* (Westchester, IL.: Crossway, 1987). [Moody professor. provides Scriptural analysis.]

Elwell, Walter A., gen. ed., *Baker Encyclopedia of the Bible* (Grand Rapids: Baker, 1988).

Foster, Neill K., *Warfare Weapons* (Camp Hill, PA: Christian Publications, 1995).

——, with Paul King, *Binding & Loosing – Exercising Authority over the Dark Powers* (Camp Hill, PA: Christian Publications, 1998).

Friesen, James G., *Uncovering the Mystery of MPD – Its Shocking Origins . . . Its Surprising Cure* (San Bernardino, CA: Here's Life, 1991). [*re* Multiple Personality Disorder.]

Goodman, Felicitas D., *How About Demons?* (Bloomington: Indiana University Press, 1988).

Green, Michael, *I Believe in Satan's Downfall* (London: Hodder & Stoughton, 1981).

Green, Thomas H., *Weeds Among the Wheat* (Notre Dame, Indiana: Ave Maria, 1984). [About discernment.]

Hiebert, Paul G., 'The Flaw of the Excluded Middle,' *Missiology 10* (January, 1982), 35-47.

Horrobin, Peter, *Healing Through Deliverance* (Chichester, UK: Sovereign World, 1991).

Kelsey, Morton, *Discernment: A Study in Ecstasy and Evil* (New York: Paulist Press, 1978).

Koch, Kurt, *Christian Counselling and Occultism* (Grand Rapids: Kregel, 1972).

Kraft, Charles H., *Defeating Dark Angels: Breaking Demonic Oppression in the Believer's Life* (Ann Arbor, MI: Servant Publications, 1992). [Explains addressing demons and limited conversation with them.]

SELECTED BIBLIOGRAPHY

MacMillan, John A., *The Authority of a Believer* (Harrisburg, PA: Christian Publications, 1980). [A compilation of *The Authority of the Believer* and *The Authority of the Intercessor*].

McAll, Kenneth, *Healing the Family Tree* (London: Sheldon Press, 1986). [About occult and curse inheritance.]

Miller, Elliot, *A Crash Course on the New Age* (Grand Rapids: Baker House, 1989).

Mitchell, L. David, 'Deliver Us from Evil,' *Alliance Life*, 1988, March 2: 6-9.

Montgomery, John Warwick, ed. *Demon Possession* (Minneapolis, MN: Bethany House, 1976). [Medical, Historical, Anthropological and Theological Symposium: papers presented to the Christian Medical Association.]

—— *Principalities and Powers* (Minneapolis: Bethany Fellowship, 1981).

Murphy, Ed., 'We Are at War', in Peter C. Wagner and Douglas Pennoyer, eds., *Wrestling with Dark Angels* (Ventura, CA.: Regal Books, 1990).

—— *The Handbook for Spiritual Warfare* (Nashville: Nelson, 1992). [Unmatched for volume of material in one book.]

Neil-Smith, Christopher, *The Exorcist and the Possessed* (St. Ives, England, James Pike, 1974).

Penn-Lewis, Jessie, with Evan Roberts, *War on the Saints* (n.d., Ninth Edition, Unabridged, New York: Thomas E. Lowe, 1973). [Note: Avoid the abridged edition. It destroys the basis of the original work.]

Powlison, David, *Power Encounters – Reclaiming Spiritual Warfare* (Grand Rapids: Baker Books, 1995). [Challenges deliverance concepts.]

Ryrie, Charles C., *Basic Theology* (Wheaton: Victor, 1981).

197

Sargant, William, *Battle for the Mind* (London: Heinemann, 1957).

Scanlon, Michael & Randall J. Cirner, *Deliverance from Evil Spirits: A Weapon for Spiritual Warfare* (Ann Arbor, MI: Servant Books, 1980). [Helpful Roman Catholic treatment.]

Southard, Samuel and Donna, 'Demonizing and Mental Illness (III): Explanations and Treatment, Seoul,' *Pastoral Psychology* 35:1 (Fall 1986), 132-51.

Steyne, Philip M., *Gods of Power – A Study of the Beliefs and Practices of Animists* (Houston, TX.: Touch Publications, 1989).

Thayer, Joseph Henry, *Greek-English Lexicon of the New Testament* (Grand Rapids: Baker, 1977).

Unger, Merrill F. *Demons in the World Today* (Wheaton: Tyndale, 1971). [Dallas Seminary professor who became protagonist for deliverance ministry.]

—— *What Demons Can Do to Saints* (Chicago: Moody, 1991).

Wagner, C. Peter & F. Douglas Pennoyer, eds., *Wrestling with Dark Angels* (Ventura, CA: Regal Books, 1990). [Came out of a symposium of evangelicals, charismatics and Pentecostals.]

Wagner, C. Peter, *Engaging the Enemy: How to Fight and Defeat Territorial Spirits*, (Ventura, CA: Regal, 1991). [Evangelism and mission focus.]

—— *Warfare Prayer: How to Seek God's Care and Protection in the Battle to Build His Kingdom* (Ventura: Regal, 1992).

Warner, Timothy M., *Spiritual Warfare* (Westchester, IL: Crossway, 1991). [Good teaching, includes a missionary slant.]

Watson, David, *The Hidden Battle* (Wheaton: Harold Shaw, 1980).

White, Thomas B., *The Believer's Guide to Spiritual Warfare* (Ann Arbor, MI: Servant Publications, 1990). [Basic teaching.]

Wimber, John with Kevin Springer, *Power Evangelism – Signs and Wonders Today* (London: Hodder and Stoughton, 1985).

—— *Power Healing* (San Francisco: Harper & Row, 1986).

What others are saying about *Liberty in Jesus*:

'*Liberty in Jesus* should be a significant contribution to the renewal of North American Evangelism.'
Dr Arnold L. Cook,
President, The Christian and
Missionary Alliance in Canada.

'We seldom address the reality of evil with a balanced, Biblical, Christ-centered approach, as David Mitchell does so well!'
Rev. James K. Wagner, *Senior Pastor,*
Fairview United Methodist Church, Dayton, Ohio.

'Here is a practical guide book for all those who take Jesus' instructions about deliverance seriously. This book adds a valuable diagnostic dimension for seeing people's problems from a much neglected Biblical and clinical perspective.
Dean Hochstetler, *Ordained Minister*
of Deliverance, The Mennonite Church.

'David Mitchell has captured the essence of the deliverance ministry in an accountable and Christ-adoring manner – read with profit!'
Dr K. Neill Foster, *President/Publisher,*
Christian Publications, Inc.

'. . . most interesting and clearly presented . . . obviously blessed with good discernment.'
Dr Timothy Warner, author, *Spiritual Welfare:*
Victory Over the Powers of this Dark World.